Jan Messent's

World of Embroidery

Jan Messent's
World of Embroidery

The Fabric of Thoughts

B T Batsford Ltd, London

Acknowledgements

It would have been quite impossible to compose a book of this nature without the help of the many people who contributed slides or photographs of their embroideries, made things and wrote about them and lent me their thoughts from as far afield as South Africa and the United States. In addition, the ideas my students gleaned from workshops have been considerable and stimulating. To all these people, I give my most sincere thanks for their generosity, cooperation and support.

First published 1996
Reprinted 1997
© Jan Messent 1996

ISBN 0 7134 7998 1

A catalogue record for this book is available from the British Library.

Published by
B T Batsford Ltd
583 Fulham Road
London SW6 5BY

Printed in Hong Kong

The embroideries, drawings and diagrams are the work of the author unless otherwise credited.

Right: *Mosaic Floor Quilt*, by Barbara Howell

Contents

Introduction

The real voyage of discovery consists not in seeking new landscapes but in having new eyes.
Marcel Proust

This book is not so much about how to design as about how to express our thoughts in a visual way that will make some sense, both to ourselves and others. It is to do with discovering links between ideas and images and learning how to use words as pegs to hang thoughts on. It includes how to use colour and symbolism to say what we feel, and how to use illusions, constructions, shapes and lines to convey messages.

Some of our thoughts are very far from being visual; indeed, those things we would like to express through our embroidery are often tucked so far back in our minds that we are not even sure they qualify as ideas at all. This book aims to help you bring these vague feelings forward, to give them substance and to explore their shapes and their potential as embroidery.

There is no one-and-only way of saying something; there is a different way for each of us, just as there will be a different effect on everyone who hears it. Here, I try to explain some of the different ways of saying things in embroidery that will lead you towards true self-expression. It will be a voyage of discovery, not only of design possibilities, but of yourself, too.

We do not see things as they are. We see them as we are.
The Talmud

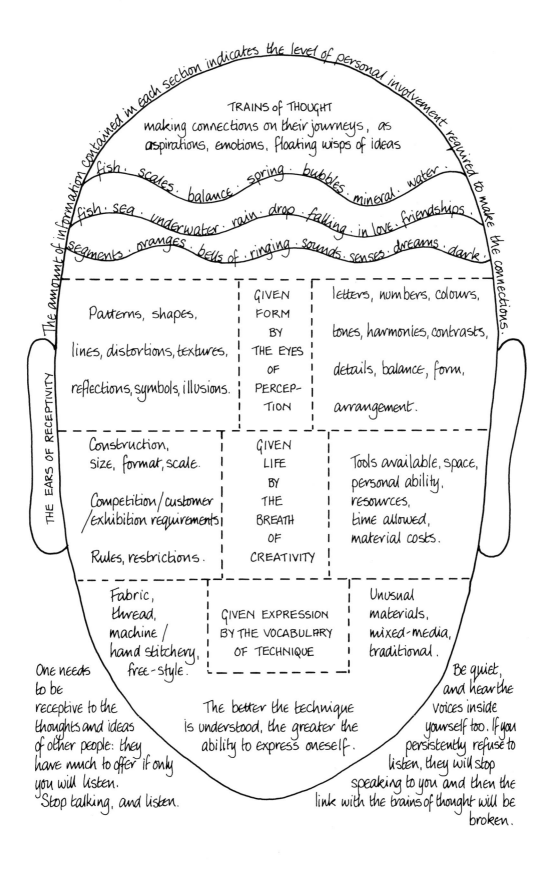

The amount of information contained in each section indicates the level of personal involvement required to make the connections.

TRAINS of THOUGHT
making connections on their journeys, as
aspirations, emotions, floating wisps of ideas

fish · scales · balance · spring · bubbles · mineral · water ·

fish · sea · underwater · rain · drop · falling · in love · friendships ·

segments · oranges · bells of · ringing · sounds · senses · dreams · dark ·

THE EARS OF RECEPTIVITY

Patterns, shapes,

lines, distortions, textures,

reflections, symbols, illusions.

GIVEN
FORM
BY
THE EYES
OF
PERCEP-
TION

letters, numbers, colours,

tones, harmonies, contrasts,

details, balance, form,

arrangement.

Construction,
size, format, scale.

Competition/customer
/exhibition requirements

Rules, restrictions.

GIVEN
LIFE
BY
THE
BREATH
OF
CREATIVITY

Tools available, space,
personal ability,
resources,
time allowed,
material costs.

Fabric,
thread,
machine /
hand stitchery,
free-style.

GIVEN EXPRESSION
BY THE VOCABULARY
OF TECHNIQUE

Unusual
materials,
mixed-media,
traditional.

One needs
to be
receptive to the
thoughts and ideas
of other people: they
have much to offer if only
you will listen.
Stop talking, and listen.

The better the technique
is understood, the greater the
ability to express oneself.

Be quiet,
and hear the
voices inside
yourself too. If you
persistently refuse to
listen, they will stop
speaking to you and then the
link with the brains of thought will be
broken.

chapter one

Word Associations

This chapter will help your imagination start to unfold as you begin to think laterally around words and concepts. There is no drawing or designing involved unless you wish it. The small sketches on page 11 are of ideas which spring to my mind as particular words appear, and illustrate how meanings can be twisted away from the conventional ones to form alternative interpretations.

Designing begins long before the drawing stage, long even before any visual ideas take form. First, you may have a feeling at the back of your mind that there is something you need to express; a message that you want to convey. At this stage, it may be vague or quite positive, but it lacks shape or form; it is only a spark. If you could write about it, that might help to give it some substance, but some things cannot be said. You want to illustrate it, except that there is nothing to see, only a feeling. To bring this feeling one step nearer to the front of your mind, you will need to look for links which will connect it to something visual. And this is where words come in.

They are not the only link, but they are the ones we shall use for these first exercises. They will not be sentences of the 'I feel this . . .' variety, but words of metaphor and simile, colloquialisms, titles and puns which have the ability to shake off one meaning and slip into another. At first glance this is going to look like a silly game, but its function is to invoke images by playing with words, to mentally ascribe pictorial translations to words of more than one meaning. Fortunately for us, the

English language is full of such words. This method may not immediately produce a design possibility; it isn't meant to. Simply see the exercise as a way of moving one step nearer to something visual by using words as picture-making tools.

Word Flows

This is to get the mind in tune: choose any noun or verb, then follow that with one to which it can be linked in meaning to form a double-barrelled word. Next, use the second of these words to form the first part of the next double, and so on. For example, take the word 'letter'. Now link it as follows: Letter-box: box-top: top-knot: knot-garden: garden-hose: hose-pipe: pipe-dream: dream-land: land-mark: mark-time: time-out: out-post. As you can see, we're almost back to the word 'letter' again.

Follow the same process with several different starter-words, making your list as long as you can (you may wish to have someone to help you at the beginning), but don't feel that you must bring your word full-circle to the original one each time. Now look closely at your list of words to discover how many meanings, other than the usual ones, there are. Remember: the ordinary, everyday, common meaning is *not* what you want. Twist every word and word-pair around in your head to find alternative meanings from the one in front of you. So, a letter-box as you usually see it in the door or at the post office is *out*; that's too usual. Ask yourself what else the word(s) could mean. It will become clear that not every pair of words will be useful. However you try, some will provoke no response at all. This is quite alright; just ignore these. You will see by my analysis below that the same thing happened to me. However, quite a few interesting multiple-meanings emerged. As you go over your completed list, make a note of which ones have potential, as I have done, writing down any alternative meanings as well. If you wish, a small sketch may be even more helpful. Go through my list below, noting the visual ideas which came to light simply by my juggling with the meaning of the words. This was my analysis:

Letter-box: a box containing letters of the alphabet, perhaps a child's toy with envelopes on the sides.
(box: also a shrub with tiny leaves used for hedges and topiary)
Box-top: container with a topiary (box) lid; box like a shrub-container with a box (bush) lid.
Box-top: an upper garment with a design of box-leaves on it.
Box-Top: refers to the Big Top (circus tent) made in the shape of a box with three-dimensional clowns, etc. inside.

Box-top: a container (box) shaped like a spinning-top, decorated with box leaves.
Knot-garden: an outline of a huge knot with a garden scene inside; could be two- or three-dimensional.
Knot-garden: large letters filled with a continuous garden scene, edges bordered with box hedges! Conversely, leave the letters void and use the in-between spaces for the garden.
Garden-hose: fanciful socks worn in and around the garden.
Land-mark: huge bookmark shape with landscape on it.
Land-mark: open book shape covered with landscape but leaving void where bookmark rests on it.
Land-mark: similar to above but using footprint instead of a bookmark.

If your first attempt is unhelpful, try other starter words. The ones below may produce a string of link words; follow on from where I have left off.

Pay: pay-roll: roll-mop: mop-
Winter: winter-green: green-peace: peace-
Hand: hand-bag: bag-man: man-
(U.K. readers, bag-man is U.S. for tramp)

Key-Words

Another method of producing double-barrelled words is to choose a key-word (one may already have occurred to you in the previous exercise as a good one to play with) and attach to this word any others with which it is normally associated. For example, the key-word 'house' can be linked by many others.

Words that follow 'house' include:
–wife; –hold; –room; –guest; –maid;
–party; –warming; –plant; –proud;
–bound; –sparrow; –frau.

Words to go in front of 'house' include:
glass–; tree–; boat–; green–; summer–;
work–; dog–; doll's –; guest–; coffee–.

Of course, there may be many others that
you will think of. The next step is to
analyze your list to see how you can apply
the same juggling act to the words as you
did in the previous exercise. Take every
word, separately and in pairs, and dredge
out every possible meaning, even the
irreverent ones! Remember, avoid all conventional interpretations like the plague;
you are looking for an alternative meaning.
Sometimes this may be discovered by
changing the spelling. For example,
'party', changed to 'parti', means two-
coloured or variegated, as in 'parti-
coloured' or 'parti-hose'.

At the same time, try introducing figures
or other objects into the picture. Take, for
example, the word 'housebound', with
which many people will no doubt identify.
Picture an Alice-in-Wonderland situation
where a figure grows and grows inside a
shrinking, box-like house, the roof/lid
forcing her head on to her bent knees.
The house is bound up with pretty ribbons
(as a gift would be) suggesting that, from
the outside, all is desirable and in order.
The inside reveals the sense of helplessness
and captivity of the figure. This could be

treated in either a light-hearted or serious
manner, according to whichever you felt
was appropriate.

Other images spring to mind with
'henhouse' where I see two things: first, a
wooden henhouse or frame where, instead
of real hens sitting in rows on the perches,
women sit with their legs dangling.
Second, I imagine a doll's house construction with women busy as normal inside,
but with wire-netting stretched across the
front as in a coop.

Revealing, isn't it? The point of the
exercise is to see how far these word-
connections can be used as vehicles for
already-germinating ideas relating to our
own feelings. It may be quite tempting at
this stage to pick up an idea which is
almost complete in visual content, but it is
probably better in the long term to hold
on to the idea for a while and turn it
around in your mind, make a note of it,
and then read on.

You may like to use the following as key-
words to see how many links you can find.
Make lists of words that go with each, and
then analyze them.

Family: (tree, circle, gathering . . .)
Life: (boat, cycle, buoy . . .)
Cross: (bow, purposes, patch . . .)
Out: (post, look, side . . .)

Try these words as the second ones of
a pair, as well as the first. Consider, for
example, what a 'closely-knit' family
might look like . . .

Right:
Word Associations

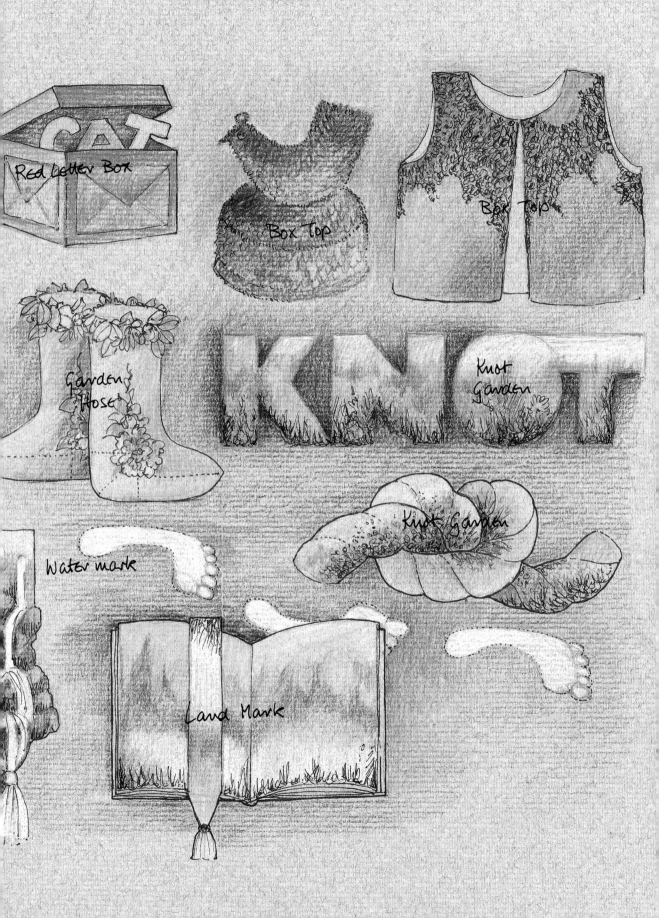

Red Letter Box

Box Top

Box Top

Garden Hose

KNOT

Knot Garden

Knot Garden

Water mark

Land Mark

Pair Bonding
by Kay Greenlees

Kay Greenlees' work is always highly personal and perceptive, drawing ideas from personal relationships, feelings and reactions to her environment and society in general. Kay describes *Pair Bonding* as a perceptive look at town-life: the crowds, the buildings, the way people adapt to limited space and the barriers they use to delineate that space. The figures merge into their painted background yet they are, in fact, raised from that surface by appliqué, then machine embroidered.

There are also further meanings implied by the words of the title. 'Pair-bonding' can also refer to the process during which some birds and animals seek each other out with a view to a permanent relationship. This is a serious and time-consuming business consisting of rituals, refusals, acceptances and sometimes misunderstandings. 'Bonding' is also the name given to the method of bricklaying in a variety of patterns made by the long and short sides of the bricks.

Pair Bonding,
by Kay Greenlees
Paint, mixed media,
machine embroidery,
and appliqué
*Alan and Viv Goddard's
collection*

Double-Duty Words

These are similar in function to key-words, the only real difference being in their source. Instead of deliberately taking a key-word and using it to generate new words, double-duty words lie waiting to be discovered all around you. As your mind becomes more receptive, they will appear to pop into it from nowhere, though in reality they seep into your consciousness from your environment. You read them, hear them, see them as shop signs or book titles and say them by accident, often with hilarious results. As with the key-word exercise, the idea is deliberately to confuse the meanings, as a child might do unintentionally. To come under this heading, either one or both of the words in the pair must have more than one meaning.

Use the following suggestions as examples, then discover some of your own and make notes about the ideas which emerge. Remember, this is only an exercise in seeing things differently; if it actually produces ideas for design, that is a bonus, not a requirement.

Foot-print

Usual meaning: mark left by shoe or bare foot.
Print – as seen in books and newspapers, calligraphy, capital letters.
Print – as in screen-printing, potato-print, pattern-making.

Alternatives:
a Wet sand or grass pattern inside a foot-shape.
b As above, seen inside the pattern of a shoe-sole. Could be an all-over pattern.
c Shoe-print showing sections of country-side or landscape. Could be reversed to show voids where shoe pattern is.
d Patterns of newsprint/lettering with bare foot prints and/or shoe prints. Call it 'Newsprint' instead.
e Shoe uppers, or slippers, covered with black-and-white newspaper patterns.

Pigeon-hole

Usual meanings: holes in buildings where pigeons nest; compartments in desks for letters, etc.

Alternatives:
a Letters (envelopes or alphabet) stacked into holes in a wall (with pigeons too, perhaps?)
b Desk compartments with pigeons roosting inside.

Dove-cote

Usual meaning: safe place where doves are housed. 'Cote' can become 'coat'.

Alternative:
series of fantastic coats with dove's wings, feathers, head on hood, etc. Try also 'bird-bath' and 'bird table' (birds = women).

As you become familiar with these double-duty words, you will find that you start looking for them in conversation, in reading-matter, and wherever you go during the day. They will also appear (maddeningly!) just as you are about to fall asleep. Keep a note of them as they occur. Avoid gimmicky and over-worked ideas and clichés; there are plenty of more unusual alternatives. Newspapers abound with puns and word-play titles; watch out for shop-signs too, which are often very clever. These are just a few of the many that I have noticed:

Curl up 'n' Dye (a hairdresser)
Cross Purposes (a Christian bookseller)
Knickerbox (an underwear shop)
Fresh Aire (a hairdresser in my own village, situated on the river Aire).

Here is one more phrase to ponder over:

Sheet music
Usual meaning: music that is printed on unbound pages.

Alternative:
Bed-linen embroidered with musical instruments or symbols; perhaps a quilt.

From the alternative ideas which emerge, you will see that this exercise can be used in two ways. One of these is as a way of finding a title and then using this to spark off an idea. The other is as a starting or jumping-off point for other ideas; these may be generated by something which flickers through the mind as you make notes on the double-duty words. If you find that your thoughts are suddenly developing along more interesting or deeper lines than all this, follow them and don't let them out of your sight.

Conservation
by Jan Messent

I began by analyzing the following words.

Conserve: to keep from change or decay; preserve, maintain; jam, preserved fruit.
Conservation: protection; management of natural resources and environment.
Conservatory: greenhouse for nurturing tender plants.

By deliberately confusing the meanings of the words (including the similar word 'preserve'), pictures of fruity confections begin to form which blend into the decorative shape of a greenhouse. The hexagonal package around a jar of plum conserve was the starting-point for this design. Opened out flat, it looked like a conservatory with panels and upper lights. The branch of plums appears on the surface and then disappears into the window as a silhouette, as plants do when seen from the outside. Associated words helped to focus my mind on the hidden meanings.

The embroidery was made to the same size as the package, with simple surface stitchery and couched, twisted gauze.

Right:
Conservation sketch

Next spread:
Detail of Conservation, by Jan Messent
29 x 24 cm
(11 ¹/₂ x 9 ¹/₂ in)

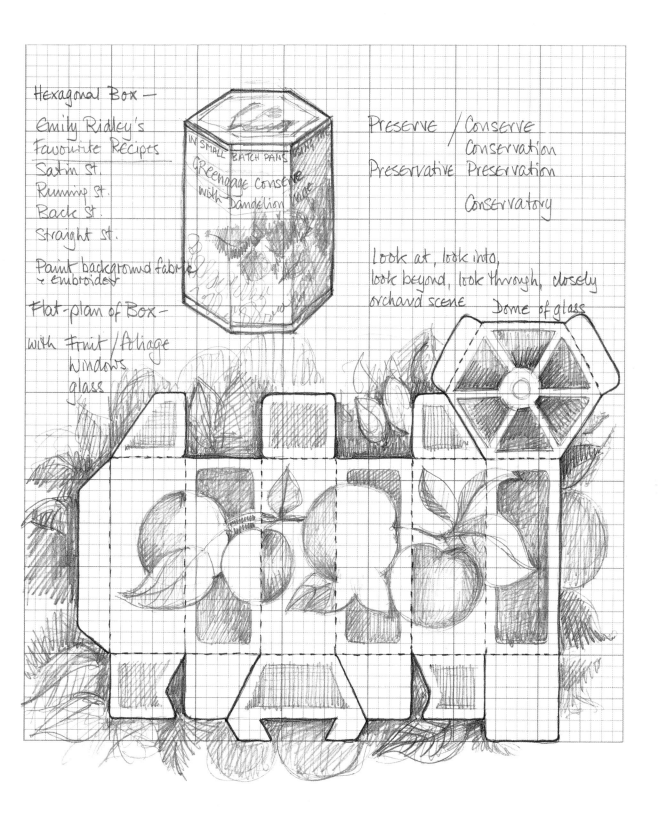

Hexagonal Box —

Emily Ridley's
Favourite Recipes
Satin St.
Running St.
Back St.
Straight St.

Paint background fabric
+ embroider

Flat-plan of Box —

with Fruit / Foliage
Windows
glass

IN SMALL BATCH PANS
GReengage Conserve
with Dandelion wine

Preserve / Conserve
Conservation
Preservative Preservation
Conservatory

Look at, look into,
look beyond, look through, closely
orchard scene   Dome of glass

Double-Duty Expressions

The double-duty expression begins with a word or phrase which requires the addition of one or more words to complete it and give it a particular meaning. These two examples show how it works. Each time, a key-word or phrase is taken and built upon to form new expressions:

Point: point of no return; point of order; beside the point; bonus points; point of fact; come to the point; make a point; setting/freezing/boiling point; score a point; stretch a point; point blank; point out; a case in point.

Line: crossing the line; hard lines; line of direction; life line; line by line; toe the line; line of duty; not in my line; line up; fall into line; read between the lines.

Apply to these expressions the same treatment you applied to double-duty words, ie. twist the meaning away from its usual one. In the first example above, I tried to 'see' it by changing the word 'point' from 'the point of an argument' to a visual point in space. If the meaning is semi-visual, as in 'line of direction', try to see this as even more visual and decorative than it really is. The double-duty expressions often go further towards a visual conception than single or double words do. The pictures here are what sprang into my mind as I checked through the words. See if you can tell what the titles are before turning the book upside-down to find out.

Here is another double-duty expression full of potential ideas:

Out of . . . line; tune; sorts; luck; control; pocket; joint; shape; stock; my hands; trouble; play; favour; key; step; character; season; proportion; steam; breath; action; turn; doors; office; harm's way; date; fashion/vogue; keeping; love; context; reach; depth; work; focus; print; this world.

Beware of interpreting a phrase which is already visual in its usual context. For example, 'out of proportion' and 'out of focus' are already visual ideas and so to use these in quite a different way would require more than the usual amount of ingenuity on your part. If this cannot be done, leave them alone and go on to another phrase which offers more scope.

As you make a list of words to complete the phrase, roll them around together in your mind to test them for any extra

Below (clockwise, from top left):
Setting point; point blank; lifeline; reading between the lines

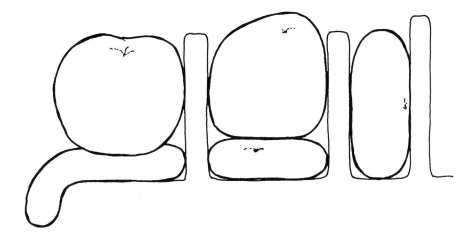

Above:
**Sketch of
stone and metal
sculpture**
Norwich press offices

meanings. It is quite likely that several will appeal to you for all kinds of unconscious reasons, and also that some will have to be discarded immediately. 'Out of steam', for instance, seems to me to suggest kettles and railways and very little else, whereas 'out of print' means much more because the word 'print' is an adaptable, decorative one, open to several interpretations.

This exercise, like the other word-associations, brings you a few steps nearer to being able to visualize things which were originally just words or figures of speech. In fact, by now you will be beginning to see things emerge which were previously mere abstractions in your mind. By using them in a different way, and applying new rules of the game, you will begin to see pictures. Some of these will have nothing whatever to do with the original meaning; that doesn't matter at all. But some of them may still have the remains of the original meaning clinging to them. When this happens – when you can give your visual idea more than one meaning, as in Kay Greenlees' *Pair Bonding* (see page 12) – then it becomes even more interesting.

All of this requires no special talent; it is a way of thinking laterally which can be practised every day. We see and hear examples of it all around us. Comedians thrive on it, newspapers demand it, writers fall into its trap unwittingly!

'Her eyes fell to the floor.' 'His gaze swept the room.' 'May I press you to a jelly?' 'They had to fall back on an alternative solution'. And so on; no doubt you are remembering many other figures of speech you have heard.

Keep your ears tuned towards more picturesque speech.

Note: you will find a copy of *Roget's Thesaurus* very useful to look up words relating to each other in meaning, as well as the *Brewer's Dictionary of Phrase and Fable* (see Bibliography, page 140).

The symbolic stone and metal sculpture shown above is to be found outside the press offices in Norwich, England. It is not as totally abstract as it appears to be on first sight. The golden apples, symbolizing knowledge and wisdom, are trapped between upright columns which are able to control, restrict, organize, categorize, suppress or distort. The word 'press' is therefore being used in both senses. However, there is still an opportunity for freedom, upwards.

Fragments,
by Jan Messent
18 x 13 cm (7 x 5 in)

Fragments
by Jan Messent

Bits and pieces emerged from a drawer which I was turning out, but I didn't want to throw them away as they brought back memories and fragments of lost times, partly sweet and partly painful. I found a pressed leaf, tiny scraps of precious fabrics, a button, part of a tortoise-shell earring and a feather. In their assembled form, they still evoke memories. The word 'fragments' is embroidered freehand in a space-dyed cotton.

Other fragments which could be applied quite simply in this way could include pieces of postcards and old photographs, jewellery, hair, cords, ribbons and lace handkerchiefs, wedding-cake decorations, pressed flowers, theatre tickets, train tickets, letters, children's drawings (re-embroidered), tiny toys, butterfly wings – all kinds of precious broken bits.

Word Circles

This particular method of connecting ideas to a key-word is a highly productive and revealing exercise. During the previous exercises, a certain word or phrase may have caught your attention as being worthy of deeper investigation. This will no doubt be something which could be channelled into various different directions – avenues of thought, as we call them. But how can you explore all the different avenues simultaneously without getting lost?

To form a word circle, the key-word is written in the centre of a large blank sheet of paper. Around this word the various avenues of thought are then constructed like the spokes of a wheel, little by little. New connecting words are allotted their proper spoke according to the context, as you will see in the examples. Write down each word or phrase that springs to mind as a result of your thinking around the key-word, exploring all its connections, implications and connotations. If a new word doesn't fit properly on any of the existing spokes (i.e. if it is out of context), create a new one for it. Again, a thesaurus will help you to find new relevant words.

For a first word circle experiment, try a word like 'sea', starting off with associated words such as: waves; ripples; reflections; patterns; spray; fish; shells; underwater life; mermaids and men; swimmers; boats, buoys and ships; lighthouses; oil-rigs; harbours; tides; piers and pavillions; shoreline; holiday snaps.

Left:
Word circle – Fragment

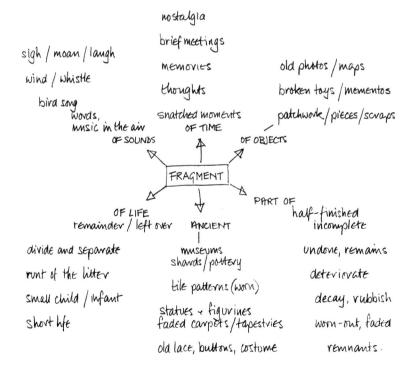

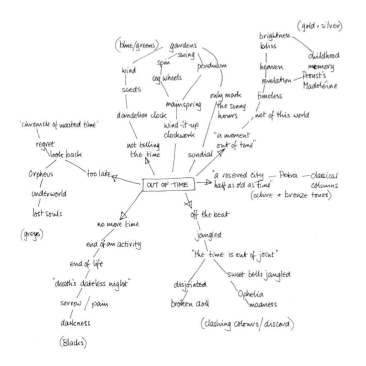

The word circle contains the following handwritten associations radiating from the central key-word:

(gold + silver)
brightness
bliss
childhood
memory
Proust's
Madeleine
(blue/greens) gardens
swing
spin
pendulum
heaven
wind
cog wheels
revelation
seeds
only mark
the sunny
hours
mainspring
timeless
not of this world
dandelion clock
wind-it-up
clockwork
"chronicle of wasted time"
regret
not telling
the time
"a moment
out of time"
look back
sundial
Orpheus
too late
OUT OF TIME
"a rosered city
half as old as time" — Petra — classical
columns
(ochre + bronze tones)
underworld
lost souls
no more time
off the beat
(greys)
end of an activity
jangled
end of life
"the time is out of joint"
"death's dateless night"
sweet bells jangled
disjointed
Ophelia
madness
sorrow / pain
broken doll
darkness
(clashing colours/discord)
(Blacks)

Above:
Word circle –
Out of Time

It is important to remember that the key-word represents the basic thought or idea which you are trying to find a way of describing. It would be all too easy, when words like 'garden' or 'shell' appear on one of your spokes, to think, 'Ah yes, shells, pretty shapes. Yes, I think I can do shells and call it "sea". Off we go, then'. Before you know it, another facile embroidery has appeared, demanding nothing more of the viewer than an appreciation of its prettiness and containing no meaning, hidden or otherwise. This is not what we are about.

What do you need to look for? Firstly, the key-word should be one which means something to you. You will instinctively know if it does – it will produce a different feeling in your breast or your throat, or a thought-drift into another time. Some key-words, phrases or connections will

flow from your pencil all by themselves and you may well find that the general direction of the word circle reflects deeper thoughts which were just waiting under the surface for a hook to latch on to them and bring them into the light. This is as it should be, for the key-word is there for that very purpose. Sometimes, certain words may be too painful, in which case their connections are better left undisturbed. On the other hand, you will find many light-hearted and joyful ideas that can be woven around the key-word; there is as much validity in these aspects as in any other.

We are still only dealing with words and the ideas which spring from them – you may be wondering where the designing comes in? Wait, be patient. There's some more thinking to do yet, more visualizing. If you are ultimately going to produce something which will be a part of yourself, you must be sure that the final image is not more like somebody else through lack of preparation. Look carefully at your word circle, connecting the words on the spokes to the key-word to see where the visual connections occur. It is quite certain that there will be more ideas than you can deal with on one composition so, for now, concentrate on one (or two at the most) which show definite possibilities for further development. Look at the 'fragment' word circle on page 21 and follow my train of thought:

Fragment: the nostalgia trail; bits found in a forgotten drawer; old mementos; photos; buttons; scraps of fabric, jewellery. Could make an interesting composition.

Fragmented sounds: perhaps difficult to visualize, although I may be able to convey mood using colours and textures.

Fragments of life: interesting; I wonder if this could be shown by a series of vertical lines chopping up the composition into sections; fragments like a broken thing with bits of pictures on it, slightly out of true. Divided and separate and yet one piece.

Fragments of fabric: a kind of rag-bag of incomplete pieces, embroideries that appear half-finished, connected by something which represents me – a thread, cord, or rope perhaps? Or words. Worn-out bits (of me, or my past?), tapestry of life. (That's good.) Does it have to be in fragments? Yes.

Fragments of museum bits: colourful ideas here; faded tones; ancient civilizations; could get a bit ordinary though, unless I try to combine the past with the present. Fragments of classic Greek statues; earthenware figures. Could be seen as fragments of real and unreal figures, like ghosts.

Fragments of time: parts of time-measuring equipment (research needed here) mixed in with part-faces of people I knew. Ghostly faces superimposed on clock or watch-faces, fob-watches. Thoughts shown as decorative words interlaced with fragments of other things; could be a quotation about time, or faded fragments of words, just understandable.

Fragments of thoughts: quick flashes of colour too slippery to hold on to, thoughts are like snippets of flimsy coloured fabrics, insubstantial and almost transparent (see page 106).

You will see from this string of thoughts that pictures begin to emerge when you allow your thoughts and words to roam about on the page in front of you as you look at your word circle. Whenever this happens, however vague and rambling they may be, write them down – otherwise, you will have to keep reminding yourself what it was that you thought of every time you need to compare ideas.

At this stage, you are only one move away from designing, and now you will be able to see more clearly how your ideas have developed into potential design material just through your playing with words. Anne Wallace-Hadrill's word circle around the key-word 'Time' was constructed after a workshop on theme thinking. Anne's words include several literary references which provide further paths to investigate.

Left:
Word Circle – Time,
by Anne Wallace-Hadrill

Fabrication,
by Milly Stevens
91.5 x 61cm
(36 x 24 in)
Felting, found fabrics,
mixed media and stitchery

Fabrications
by Milly Stevens

Milly allows the materials themselves to dictate the final direction of the design. She finds that ordering and re-ordering them is a major part of the work. This is, in fact, what designing means – to play with, re-arrange and organize the various elements of a piece. This may take anything from a few days to a few months and will sometimes entail a wait while the right piece turns up. Milly also uses distressing techniques, (i.e. changing the nature of the fabric by tearing, burning, etc.) as well as using paints and dyes and, when necessary, manufacturing pieces to fit.

Milly says that the subject matter is personal. It depends on her reactions to her environment, the spirit of a place, snippets of conversation, quotations, diaries of time and space and her personal mythology. Not surprisingly, therefore, the viewer is left to form a personal interpretation of the work, using their own store of personal memories sparked off by the fragments within the assemblages. Bits of garments, nets, felts, stitchery (hand and machine), hand-made papers and any other evocative debris are all recycled and re-moulded to arouse dormant memories in the viewer.

Mycenae
by Barbara Siedlecka

Trained first as an illustrator, Barbara Siedlecka now works in a variety of media including embroidery, hand-made papers and any material which will express in a spontaneous way the ideas which lie in her subconscious. These ideas are then coaxed out of the textured surface into low relief and sometimes enhanced by applied pigments. If the results are exciting enough, Barbara continues to work with them; if not, they are recycled.

Mycenae epitomizes this free way of working, bringing to the surface the ancient images of a lost civilisation. Ghostly faces appear in the flaking paint of roughened walls and tiled floors, appearing and disappearing as the textures catch the light and hold the image before it moves away again.

Mycenae,
by Barbara Siedlecka
35 x 25 cm
(14 x 10 in)
Handmade papers, stained,
laminated and embossed

Picturing the Abstract

There is an immense usefulness in the considera-tion of lines, angles and figures, because without them natural philosophy cannot be understood. They are applicable in the universe as a whole and in its parts, without restriction . . . whether as applied to matter or sense . . . For all causes of natural effects can be discovered by lines, angles and figures, and in no other way can the reason for their action possibly be known.
Robert Grosseteste, Bishop of Lincoln

Although the Bishop of Lincoln was actually referring to geometry rather than purely abstract line and shape, his reflec-tions are just as relevant to our kind of designing, 'whether as applied to matter or sense . . .' Lines and shapes have in-built meanings which are so deeply rooted in our consciousness that it would be difficult to shake off or ignore them. Whether we choose to make use of this fact or not, the direction and quality of lines and shapes will evoke certain responses, just as surely as words will. If understood by the design-er, they can do much to carry messages deep into the heart of the viewer. Chapter Seven on Symbolism has more to say on this topic but here we will link the use of lines and shapes to words.

So far, we have looked at ways of wring-ing the last drop of meaning from words, not allowing the obvious interpretation to stand in our way. In this exercise, we choose words which may have a pictorial image in common usage but which have an abstract meaning as well. For instance, the word 'peace' is usually linked to scenes of tranquillity and soft, gentle colours. But it also signifies an abstract emotional or physical state, a feeling inside ourselves that is not visual. Does this mean that because in this last context it can't be seen, it can't ever be expressed, except using pictorial imagery? You may remember having seen an image somewhere; a line, shape or colour which typified for you at that moment a feeling of repose and peace. These lines would no doubt have been soft, gentle, perhaps undulating, in harmonic colours and subdued tones. These abstract images are described in 'peaceful' words. Apart from those just mentioned, there are many others which could be used to describe the feeling of peace without the need to draw a realistic picture.

As another example, take the word 'tangle'. In daily life this is often associa-ted with a pile of ropes, yarns, clothes or spaghetti, but it also has abstract connota-tions when used to describe a state of mind, a social situation or a point in life when one's ideas must be sorted out before progress can be made. In terms of lines and shapes, this would no doubt follow a similar form to the tangle of ropes or fabrics – you would not need to be spe-cific about the actual form, though other images could be enmeshed in the tangle to imply the kind of tangle it was, such as faces, bodies or fragments of treasures.

As an exercise, draw four two-inch squares, side by side, and label each one with a word from the following list: joy, fear, celebration, anger, loneliness, peace, fulfilment, activity. Now, without using any pictures, images or traditional symbols of any kind but only lines and shapes of an abstract nature, take a pencil and let it por-tray the chosen word within each square.

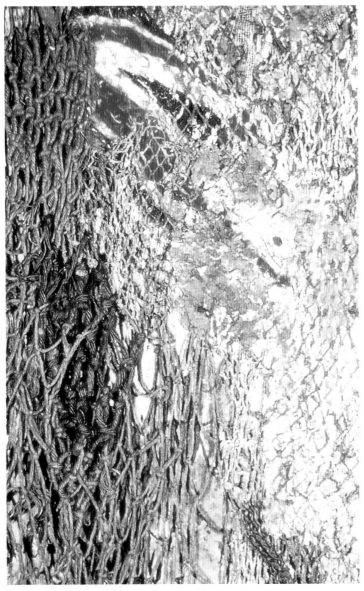

All at Sea,
by Milly Stevens
1.2 x 0.9 m (4 x 3 ft)

All at Sea
by Milly Stevens

This panel includes fragments of nets in a watery sea-like environment of flotsam, restlessly moving with the swell of the tides. The eye is drawn upwards by the vertical lines towards the red splash at the top, which looks like an odd refraction on the surface of the water. The title and image combine to suggest a fragmentary washed-up feeling of untogetherness and dissipated energies, something which we must all at some time have experienced.

Milly Stevens' early training was in fine art as a painter, but over the past thirteen years or so her work has combined collage with stitchery, using found and recycled materials. She especially likes to glean her local beaches for debris washed up during the stormy winter months. She has developed a good eye for small objects like pieces of blue and white china, pebbles, fossils, driftwood, rusty metal and tiny scraps of sea-eroded fabrics. Milly also collects wood, sections of fishing-nets, floats and any other flotsam and jetsam which looks as though it might be useful. Even feathers, old shoes, sails, tarpaulins and plastics are sometimes incorporated.

Quotations as Starting Points

Beyond words, beyond understanding, but not beyond feeling.
Spoken by a man on television on the eve of St. Valentine's Day, 1993.

In your word-circle, you may have found it appropriate to introduce quotations which are in some way associated with the key-word. Quotations often express succinctly and poetically what we find difficult to say. They may help to formulate images in our minds which go some way towards making an idea visual. Look particularly at books of quotations; note lines and words of special meaning that you come across in prose and poetry; and jot down song words and memorable snippets of overheard speech. Think about the general sense of the words, and ask yourself why they affect you. It may also help to analyze the quotation in the following way if you're thinking about how it could be used in design:

a   Identify and repeat the words which are most meaningful, i.e. the key-words.
b   Look for visual words which evoke pictures or images.
c   Look for words which suggest shapes, lines, textures, patterns or colour.
d   Look for words which could be replaced by symbols.

To see how this analysis works, consider the following example:

Thoughts too deep to be expressed, and too strong to be suppressed.
George Withers

a   Key-words: 'thoughts', 'deep', 'strong' – all easily connected in the mind by strong, powerful images. 'Expressed', 'suppressed' – two opposites, one which suggests letting go, the other keeping in.
b   Visual words: abstract, nothing pictorial, but images of deep, flowing things.
c   Shapes, etc.: thoughts are often referred to as 'patterns of thought' – this may be useful. Colours may be dark, suggesting depth, with some reflections – another useful link. 'Pushing' lines and shapes could be used, as well as holding-in/containing shapes and/or lines.
d   Symbols: more or less as c), but will have to decide how to represent thoughts or whether to concentrate more on the environment in which they are struggling to escape. 'Deep' and 'strong' are both positive words. Some visual conflict going on here.

Many quotations contain opposites, which can be expressed visually in a variety of ways. Consider, for example: straight – curved; static – mobile; area – line; angular – rounded; loud/hard – soft; heavy – light; smooth – rough; large – small; broad – narrow; thick – thin; dense/solid – hazy/transparent; single – plural; light – dark; high – low; inside – outside; vertical – horizontal.

When using a quotation as a starting-point, you should also consider using words as part of the actual design. Calligraphy has an important function in design; the shapes of the letters can be moulded to accentuate the mood of the subject and the words make clearer any message which the designer wishes to convey unambiguously. Letter-shapes (i.e. the words) may form the major part of the design or take on a supporting role which is secondary to the other visual images.

Here is another example of a quotation, written in memory of the writer's friend who died as a young woman:

The orb of your life is not to be so rounded; for you the crescent phase must suffice.
Charlotte Brontë

a   Key-words: 'orb', 'life', 'rounded', 'crescent phase'.
b   Visual words: mostly associated with the moon, itself a female symbol.
c   Shapes: may include circles in varying stages of completion.
d   Colours: those that symbolize youth, life and death.
e   Construction: could be contained within a circle – two- or three-dimensional. Use lettering, perhaps. The concept could be arranged in a series, beginning with the womb and ending with a circular mirror showing a young woman's face, a ring, a crystal, ripples in a pool . . . (Look for circular objects to supplement these ideas.)

The Visual Aspects of Words

Make letters reflect the meaning of the words, as though this were the only way to explain their meaning to someone who did not understand your language. It is often quite remarkable to see how easily letters can be steered in the right direction as though they were just waiting for the chance. Use capital as well as small letters and look at the variety of calligraphic styles available.

1   Make words appear and disappear by changing the tonal values.
2   Place letters upside-down or sideways, but make sure the word is still understandable.
3   Break up letters to convey words such as 'fracture', 'shatter' and 'disconnect'.
4   For other ideas, look at word-games such as crosswords, Scrabble, Eye-spy and Pictionary.

Other words and phrases which have to do with writing and printing are: special delivery; rejection-slip; last post; print run; red-letter day; block letters; reprint; out-of-print. Many of these have wonderfully visual double-meanings which can be tied in to link with your personal thoughts and ideas.

Right:
Visual words

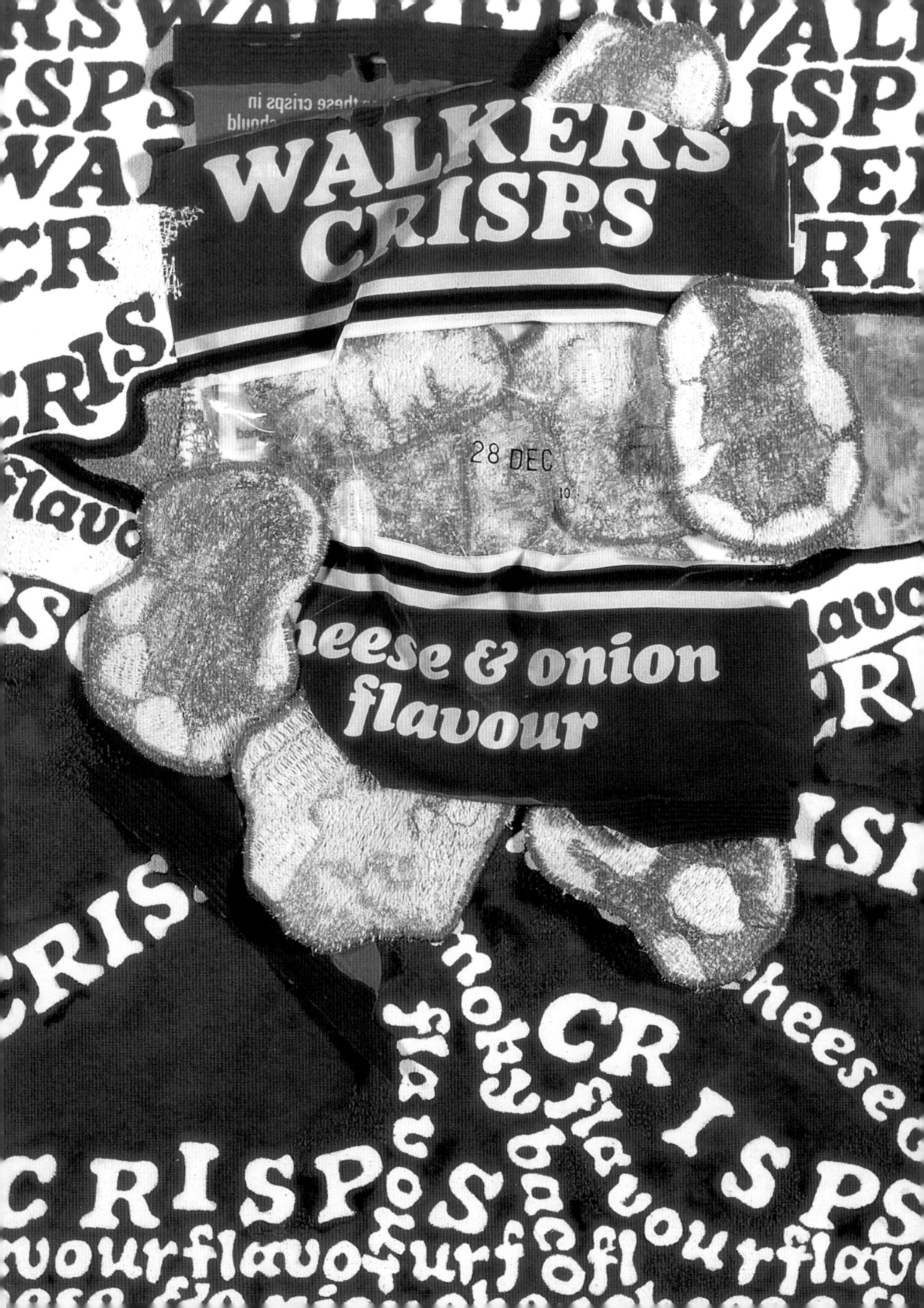
WALKERS CRISPS
heese & onion flavour
28 DEC

Yet Another Diet
by Kay Greenlees

Kay describes this panel as a straightforward challenge as to why women accept the notion of dieting and altering their bodies so readily. This panel was one of a pair on the same theme. You can almost hear the crackle of the crisp packet as the words – embroidered at different angles as though the contents had already been devoured – glare at us in reproachment.

There are many other areas where men, women and children are expected to conform to socially accepted standards of appearance and behaviour. Many of these standards are the legacies of outworn modes and traditions, though some go even deeper than that. To comment on these expectations would provide material for a lifetime's work. 'Cast-off' and 'displaced persons' might provoke more title ideas, just to get your thoughts flowing.

Yet Another Diet,
by Kay Greenlees
42 x 33 cm
(16 $\frac{1}{2}$ x 13 in)
Paint, mixed media and
machine embroidery

Wedding Presents,
by Renate Meyer
82 x 56 cm (32 x 22 in)
Watercolour on white
cotton, bonded on to grey
polyester which is both
painted and stitched to give
an appearance of depth

Wedding Presents
by Renate Meyer

Renate Meyer's Jewish family fled to England in the early 1930's to escape persecution from Nazi Germany. Renate was then evacuated from London as a nine-year-old child; this traumatic event only added to her insecurity. Her ready assimilation of English standards was a cause of much misunderstanding between herself and her family who still spoke German at home, ate continental food and kept a tight hold of their old customs and traditions.

Against considerable opposition, Renate went to art school and fell in love. Her decision to marry met with dismay and outright hostility from her family, for Charles Keeping was a typical angry young man of no means and from an entirely different social and cultural background. Misunderstandings between the now extended family abounded. Neither did the appearance of children help the situation. And while her husband struggled to make a living from illustrating, Renate struggled to balance her role of loving wife and mother with that of dutiful daughter.

It was only in later years that Renate felt the urge to communicate these memoirs through paint and fabric. *The Life Cycle*, as depicted in a huge wall-tray of soft-sculptured apples which change from ripeness to decay, is one such piece. Another project is *Temptation*, which depicts plates of wicked food, embroidered so exquisitely that one might be tempted to lift off a glacé cherry, were it not under glass. Words of guilt are stitched on to the plates and tablecloth, uncomfortably reminding the viewer of more than one of the seven deadly sins.

Renate's *Life Style* project now occupies a complete room in her home, part of which is also given over to a display of her late husband's works. The conflicting years of her earlier life are now documented in paint, soft-sculpture and embroidery in which stitched writing plays an important role, as Renate believes that words help to explain the personal symbolism of the pieces. *Wedding Presents* is part of the same project, only one of the very many other pieces which overlap like a frieze around the room. This particular piece deals largely with the dilemma of marrying out of one's culture and background, a situation in which the fault lies in a lack of understanding. The buffer is the one who understands both sides and strives to hurt neither party.

This may sound like a great deal of angst, but the display also contains much humour, many poignant musings, a little gentle cynicism and a large helping of honesty so refreshing that it brings both laughter and tears very close to the surface. A therapy for the artist, certainly, but also for the viewer.

chapter two

The Use of Colour

Although colour is but one aspect of the larger subject of symbolism, it is important enough to be considered alone. Its influences are among the strongest for embroiderers. Not only can colour be one of the most important elements in conveying a message, but it also has the power to suggest – something which may or may not be picked up by the viewer. Consider the following, seen on a large card against Autumn-dressed models in a shop window in September 1992:

autumn mists harvest festivals nuts and rich pickings sharp gust of wind bonfires and fireworks fruit of labour fruits of the earth long shadows bronze copper dry green and deep red slumber to the evening ahead

As the words above demonstrate, we can be drawn into a picture of great vividness by an assortment of words. In the same way, we can be drawn into a design of some complexity by an assortment of colours which have a meaning, even if the specific meaning is not fully understood by the viewer. We react to colours in varied ways and many of these reactions are innate, stemming from a programming beyond our understanding.

In the West, some colours are known for their apparent attributes of warmth, coolness, or anonymity, mostly by association with their counterparts in the sun, water and earth. Not surprisingly, other countries have different attributes for colours. They may relate to light, power and social conditions, or to the climate and the colour of the earth. So what may mean one thing to a person from one culture may mean something entirely different to someone from another. However, as far as conveying a message or implying a

meaning is concerned, there are helpful, generally accepted routes to follow. You can ignore or flout them, but it is worth knowing about them as, after all, you cannot intelligently break rules unless you first know what they are.

It is not my intention to discuss colour theory in depth. This has already been done comprehensively elsewhere. But I do advise those who believe their innate sense of colour is sufficient to carry them through, to think seriously about spending a few days, weeks or even months getting to grips with the theory of the subject. There is no substitute, and your creative abilities will only improve as a result. It is also a good method of ridding yourself of much disinformation which you may have carried around for years. Childhood experiences of colour stay in our minds and refuse to budge until we recognize them and set them free. Similarly, what we are told about colour in our youth may inhibit our colour development well into old age – if we allow it to. I can remember being given colour advice by knowing relatives which I accepted at the time and believed to be gospel, until much later in life when I worked things out for myself. The fact that they knew nothing about art or colour seemed not to weigh with me at the time, and I suppose that, if green had not rhymed with 'seen', their advice might have been quite different!

Colour Effects

Something to note: look at the effect of your colours from the distance at which they will ultimately be seen by viewers. It often happens that the colours that previously worked together and balanced during the designing and working processes suddenly disappear or do other strange things when seen from a distance. Those little stitches of contrasting colours may lend a vividness which works well at close quarters, but they may be reduced to a grey mass as you move away. Colours must be seen and studied at various distances and in different light conditions to have the effects you intend them to have.

'Wrong' Colours

The use of so-called 'wrong' colours can suggest special conditions of light or atmosphere to a viewer, or an emotional intensity which would be missed if the subject were presented in a more conventional manner. For instance, a figure with a bright red or purple face would convey more instantly the impression of rage or embarrassment than one wearing the normal peachy-pink hue. Baking heat, discomfort, unhappiness, discord, peace

and jealousy can all be implied by upsetting the conventional colouring of things and replacing normal colours for ones which are symbolic of certain attributes (and this does not only apply to human faces). We accept this convention in modern art, where it is often used. These odd colours are not selected arbitrarily but for the purpose of adding more information to get a message across to the viewer. Embroiderers have the advantage of being able to add texture and constructional aids (see Chapter Three, page 50).

Opposites

Meaning can also be increased by placing colour-opposites (i.e. complementaries) together in a design. A small dab, patch or stitch of a complementary colour added to a relatively large area will help make a colour-scheme more intense. Indian miniature paintings of the early Eighteenth Century are often divided into areas of quite unrealistic colours, sometimes very brilliant, intended to evoke passionate responses in viewers. Specific colours were used to which viewers were meant to respond immediately, these often being opposites and discords.

Discords

Discords occur when colours placed next to each other in a design are out of their tonal order. Take any two colours, one from each side of the colour-wheel – for example, violet and orange. In their usual state, violet is darker than orange, but if this order is reversed so that the violet becomes pale and the orange dark, the result is known as a discord. The further apart on the colour-wheel the two chosen colours lie, the greater the discord when they are placed next to each other. This effect can be used to advantage to create feelings of disturbance, anxiety, unease, intrusion or dominance in a design.

Harmonies

Those colours which lie closely together on the colour-wheel (analogous colours) are said to harmonize, implying a feeling of rightness, peace and tranquillity. But for many people, this combination is a manifestation of their own inability to handle anything other than safe schemes, and can lead to dullness rather than serenity. See the note on page 35 about complementary colours and the use of opposites. Harmony should not be confused with ordinariness; feelings of harmony and peace should not be dull or unimaginative.

Warm and Cool Colours

To term certain colours as 'warm' and 'cool' is often confusing because, I believe, this relies too heavily on a literal interpretation and misses out the fact that some so-called 'cool' colours may be anything but cool when set in the right conditions, and vice-versa. While allowing for the fact that personal feelings and reactions influence the way we think about colours, the description 'warm' is general enough to be understood as referring to those colours associated with heat, fire, the sun and blood, whereas 'cool' usually refers to those associated with the sky, mists, water, ice, air and distance. The terms become useful when we want to give a blanket description to a scheme with which we

are trying to produce a certain reaction, so that one might talk about a 'cool' scheme of colours for an ice-maiden's costume, but a 'warm' scheme for a scene of a heated argument.

Advance and Recede

Closely linked to the warm and cool descriptions, we also say that some colours advance while others recede. Look at the spots of red and blue on their backgrounds of opposites to see how this happens. The colour which catches our eye first and appears to come forward to greet us is, as it happens, the warmer of the two. The one which is quieter and further away from us is the cooler one. It appears to stay behind somewhat, either as a hole or as a single piece slipped behind the red dot. It should be noted that the six colours shown on the colour-wheel are not the only examples of warm and cool colours; there are many stages in between, just as there are many ways of warming up cool colours and of cooling down warm ones by adding their opposites.

Knowing how these colours attract attention, or do not, is rather like understanding the difference between extrovert and introvert people. Colours, like people, can be mixtures of dark and light, warmth and coolness, advancing and holding back, as in a conversation or a dance. Once you begin to understand the ways in which colours behave, ideas for design can be expressed more coherently.

Splendour

A look at the paintings of the early Renaissance, Byzantine mosaics and stained

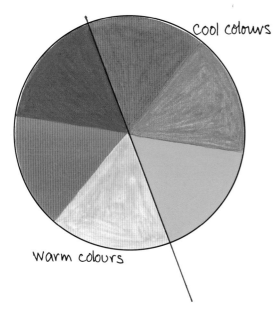

cool colours

warm colours

Colour Opposites

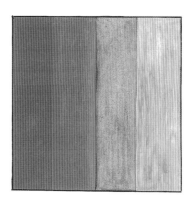

Equals

Unequals: suggests intrusion, imbalance, an outsider.

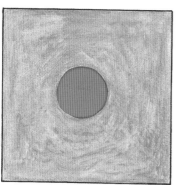

The red spot appears to come forward away from the blue background; the blue spot appears to drop back into the red background, like a hole. The red advances, the blue recedes.

Discords

This discord is greater 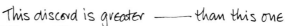 than this one

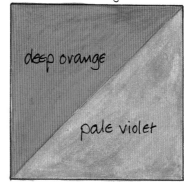

deep orange

pale violet

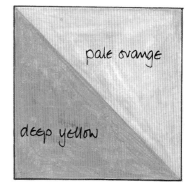

pale orange

deep yellow

glass windows will show how illusions of splendour and richness were conveyed in other media hundreds of years ago. Rich and costly paints and gold leaf invested altar-pieces, panels and icons with a beauty befitting the subjects. Wealthy donors often stipulated the exact quality and quantity of materials to be used, thus letting it be seen that they were not stinting in their gifts to the church. To achieve a rich luminosity, a gold ground would sometimes be laid, over which coloured paint was then placed, allowing the gold to filter through. Light shining through painted glass also has this luminous effect, as have the jewel-like mosaics where tiny tessarae are packed closely together, glittering and vibrant. These works of art are well worth studying in relationship to the art of embroidery, as techniques for achieving splendour in paint, glass and mosaic can also be adopted when using fabric and thread.

On a more earthly level, visits to fabric shops provide new ideas for colour-combinations, as the bolts of fabrics are often stacked together accidentally, producing brilliant effects of richness and contrast. Particularly good are shops selling fabrics from Thailand and India, those specialising in fabrics for theatre costumes and oriental carpet shops.

Colour Words

We use colour words in the ordinary language of our everyday lives, often without realizing their implied (double) meanings. If we were to make a list of all those with which we are most familiar, we might find that visual images take the place of the more usual meanings. Some examples are given below, but of course the lists are almost endless:

Green: peace; gauge; grocer; sleeves; fingers; belt; eyed-monster; house; man; wood; knight; pound.
Red: tape; herring; letter-day; rag; arrows; fox; hot; sails; handed; carpet.
Blue: beard; moon; mood; bird; stocking; blood; bottle; jeans; cheese; print.
White: wash; flag; snow; ensign; milk; feathers.
Black: beetle; looks; cloud; belt; mail; list; bird.
Brown: study; stew; earth; meadow-brown butterfly.
Silver: birch; wedding; collection; fir/fur; lining; moonbeam; spoon; fish; service.
Gold: -en fleece; -en wedding; -en eagle; finger; dust; mine; crown; coast; star.

Besides these obvious colour-words, there are others whose implied meaning we recognize by association. Minerals, flowers, woods, food and animals have all lent us extra colour-descriptions to define patterns and graduations, tones and tints. If one applies to these descriptions the same kind of reverse logic we used in Chapter One, all kinds of visual ideas emerge. Take 'marmalade cat' or 'mother of pearl' – Mother of Pearl?

Others with double-meanings include: brass (money); ivory (piano keys); jade (wilted, run-down); jet (water); ginger (spice up); tortoise-shell (cat, butterfly); harlequin fish (or perhaps a pierrot fish?).

Colour Attributes

Red   Extremes of passion. Indian miniature painters often used strong red borders to suggest realms of heightened feelings. The Chinese felt red to be rather vulgar, representing violence, blood and fire, and used it sparingly. In combination with other colours it can denote spirituality and rural feelings, e.g. poppies, geraniums. Masculinity, sun, war, royalty, love, joy, energy, fire, blood, health, anger, catastrophe, fertility, evil.

Orange/red   Energising.

Orange   Fire, flames, humility, love and happiness, warmth.

Yellow   Colours connected with sunlight, radiance of love, heat and brilliance, high spirits, pride and exaltation, truth, wisdom and learning (good for study); in the West, it denotes spiritual enlightenment. Treachery, betrayal, secrecy, avarice. Yellows dulled by black or violet have a distinctly negative effect and suggest disappointment.

Yellow/greens   Suggest Spring, foliage and regrowth.

Green   Life and death, nature, growth, regeneration, hope, eternal life, resurrection. Spring, prosperity, peace, jealousy, envy.

Blue   A pacifying colour with very complex meanings evoking highly individual reactions. Sky, heaven, spirituality, water, depth, coolness, peace, serenity, sincerity, truth, intellect, authority.

Violet   Intelligence, knowledge, sorrow, nostalgia, mourning, grief.

Purple   Royalty, pomp, pride, justice, temperence; also mysterious and disturbing.

Brown   Earth, spiritual death, renunciation, penitence.

Grey/neutrals   Neutral, anonymity, humility, mourning and depression.

White   Light, sun, air, purity, innocence, chastity, holiness.

Silver   Moon, virginity, feminine principle.

Gold   Sun, enlightenment, divine power, immortality, radiance, glory, masculine principle.

Black   Death, despair, shame, grief, etc.

Black/white   Represent the negative/positive aspects; life and death, war and peace, darkness and light. Hence those creatures coloured black-and-white (e.g. the magpie) were empowered with the control of people's destinies.

Rainbow Kimono
by Jan Messent

This kimono was originally made for my daughter, who needed a healing rainbow at the time. My fantasy story which explains the idea was that I found a piece of tattered rainbow caught on a hedge as the rainbow moved away. So I took it home and laid it out flat on the table, ready to cut a kimono from it. But then I saw that it was quite transparent and, what was more, the colours had run all over the table. So what you see is the pattern of a kimono lying on a runny piece of rainbow. Framed under the glass, it could be kept still while my daughter benefitted from its healing colours.

Rainbow Kimono,
by Jan Messent
20 x 23 cm (8 x 9 in)
Canvas embroidery in silk
and cotton, with machine
appliqué and stitchery

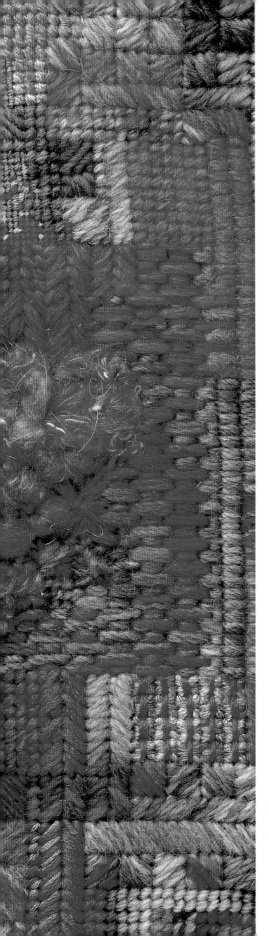

Colour Wash
by Jan Messent

The applied piece of free-style knit/crochet allows a complete mixture of colours of highly-textured yarns which could not be used to make stitches in the canvas. The same colours can, however, be allowed to move away beyond the appliqué in a more orderly fashion, picking up the same mixture of contrasts, harmonies and discords but this time in a different scale. This has the effect of leading the eye vertically, horizontally and around, in a search for connecting links of colour and texture. This is as interesting when seen from a distance as when seen close-up. The much paler tone towards the top left-hand corner holds the eye for a while, but it is then lured away towards a corresponding lightness at the extreme left and also down to the right, before being drawn round and back again.

Colour Wash,
by Jan Messent
23 x 23 cm (9 x 9 in)
Knitted and crocheted fabric
applied to canvas

Colour Exercise
by Jan Messent

Beginning at the bottom edge, with the deep blue/reds, note how one of the colours in each strip is continued into the one above it, all the way up to the gold on green at the top. This has the effect of leading the eye upwards, unconsciously seeking out the connecting colours from top to bottom. The horizontal strips help the eye move from side to side. In the inset rectangle, a small piece of canvaswork echoes the same colours on a different scale, again making the eye search for connections with the surrounding colours. From a distance, edges and colours blend, and vertical forms appear, less obvious when seen close-to. The applied piece of knit/crochet fabric on canvas effectively breaks up all the colours for just a moment.

This in fact happens when you look at any design in colour. The eye searches for connections, jumping across small gaps to link with a repeat. Having discovered one connection, it goes on to search for more, and in doing so finds other colours which link and repeat. The arrangement of colours makes the eye search the design and stay inside the framework. If something highly interesting were to be placed at one edge (such as glitter or high texture), it would hold the eye there for too long and too often, thereby stopping the eye movement around the complete area. As a designer, you may choose to do this for a particular purpose, but it should not require a vast effort of will to drag the eye away to the rest of the design. The intention is to hold the eye at specific places, not to rivet it!

Detail of Colour Exercise, by Jan Messent
29 x 28 cm (11 ¹/₂ x 11 in)
Strips of card wrapped with strips of fabric and assorted yarns

Four Changing Elements Panels
by Liz Ashurst

These four panels are based on sketches and notes made by the artist over a period of six years. They represent changes made to the environment by the rapidly increasing threat of technology to earth, air and water. The fourth element of fire is seen as a mis-used, destructive force.

The first panel, *Haystacks*, explores in vivid yellows and ochres and in the contrasting blue-violets the processing and packaging of nature.

The second panel, *Traffic*, shows the artist's concern with air pollution, as so much of our countryside is churned up for the convenience of mankind. Here, touches of the complementary red are used to add potency to the greens and greeny-yellows.

Fields of Fire, the third panel, illustrates straw and stubble being burned, with the consequent destruction of wildlife. Complementary blue-violets among the orange threads effectively make each of the colours glow with intensity.

The fourth panel, *Sea Change*, suggests the contamination of the sea by chemicals and waste products. Here again, fine threads of the colour-opposites can be seen overlaying the main blue ones, bringing alive the large expanse of solid colour into a moving wash of reflections.

Look at these four panels from a distance as well as close-up and note how the stitches of the main colours are allowed to show between the opposites, warm between cool and vice-versa.

Pages 48–49:
Seachange,
by Liz Ashurst
143 x 86 cm
(57 $^{1}/_{2}$ x 34 in)
Photograph
by Keith Harding

Haystacks,
by Liz Ashurst
143 x 86 cm
(57 ½ x 34 in)
Stitched on two sizes
of rug canvas with torn
strips of hand-dyed silk,
yarns, ribbon and cotton
Photograph
by Keith Harding

Traffic,
by Liz Ashurst
as above
Photograph
by Keith Harding

Fields of Fire,
by Liz Ashurst
as above
Photograph
by Keith Harding

chapter three

Constructions

We are so used to expressing our embroidery ideas within the usual flat, rectangular format that we often forget to investigate possible connections between the messages we are trying to convey and any implied visual constructions. This analysis of the idea while it is still in the mind is an extension of the word-play of Chapter One, where we sought extra double-meanings for words and learnt to search for associations. Here, we delve for another layer of meaning as though for a foundation on which to build; a way to present the complete idea in a format that says more about it than a simple rectangular frame would.

At the moment of writing, 'fragments' have been in vogue for some time: scrappy, frayed pieces of fabric which emphasize the ancient or antique nature of the subject. Frameless, unmounted and ragged, they embody the complete idea. At the same time, there is a swing towards completely free-standing work, which can often add weight to the meaning of a subject in a way which would be impossible in a flat panel. Apart from these, there are many other ways of presenting a message which are relatively straight-forward. This may well be a chicken-and-egg situation in which we either let a particular format or construction decide the subject, or else first find the format which will best fit the idea.

Whereas a simple rectangular frame surrounds one idea, or even a collection of ideas rolled into one design, most complex constructions are capable of carrying a whole series of interlinked ideas on different levels. The more complex the construction, the more ideas (or facets of one idea) can be illustrated. More than this,

some constructions can be made to inter-link in such a way that their component parts can be re-arranged, making a whole different set of designs possible. The creative process therefore continues long after work on the panels is completed.

Narrative embroideries and works which inform or record also have problems, the main one being concerned with how to pack a lot of information on one piece, in a way which is unified and coherent. Some of the ways in which this has been done will be examined later (see pages 60–73), for embroidery is becoming increasingly popular as a method of recording special events, such as the centenary of a city.

Make a list of ideas and words which imply a change in position and/or order, such as 'turn upside-down', 'inside out', 'back to front', etc. Begin with the ones shown here and then gradually allow yourself to add ideas of a more personal nature, things linked to the words which you feel strongly enough about to write down and consider in more detail.

Three separate sections can be turned to make different arrangements.

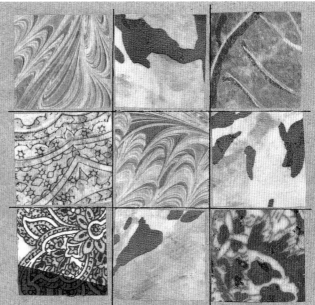

Square units made separately but designed to fit together in any arrangement, even in a line.

Vertical panels fit together in any order and any way up. The subject may be abstract or pictorial.

Curved sections can be seen horizontally or vertically, closed up or slightly separated, depending on the space. They can also be shifted slightly to make uneven edges.

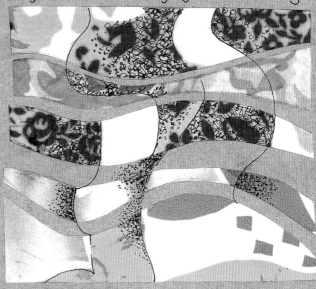

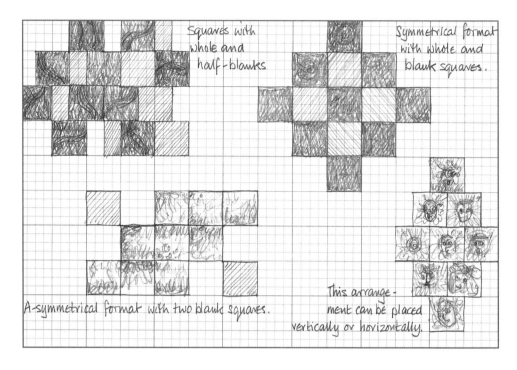

Squares with whole and half-blanks

Symmetrical format with whole and blank squares.

A-symmetrical format with two blank squares.

This arrangement can be placed vertically or horizontally.

Above:
Interchangeable units

Enlarge on these ideas, in words:

Compartment; episode; instalment; component; counterpart; phase; snippets; parting shot; fits and starts; dovetails.

Interchangeable Units

To many people, the idea of making a large or complex embroidery may be intimidating or just plain impossible due to lack of space. There are therefore good reasons for considering the idea of working in units which can later be re-grouped in a variety of formats. Separate but related design ideas can be worked on each one, combined with common elements which link or flow into each other so that whichever way up they are placed, the unity is maintained.

Another advantage is that a flexible format will fit any space available and the number of units used at any one time is for you to decide. Extra units can be added whenever you wish; likewise, they can easily be replaced or removed altogether. But the best advantage is that you can continue the designing process even after completion, for every arrangement brings a new design into focus. The diagrams here show only square units, but consider other patchwork shapes and look for words which will help the ideas to flow. Here are some words connected with the idea of changeability:

Conversion; evolution; transition; flux; turnaround; transpose; alternation; fluctuation; upheaval; diversify; metamorphosis; graduation; quantum leap; innovation.

Quarry Tiles

Deep terracotta-coloured quarry tiles are a favourite floor-covering in many older houses and can be seen in many seventeenth-century paintings of cool Dutch interiors. But for me, 'quarry tiles' has always been one of those instant double-meaning titles. In the countryside of Wharfedale, North Yorkshire, ancient disused limestone quarries are familiar sights, scattered amongst the wild hills with sheep grazing dangerously close to their edges. In my mind's eye, I see a sketchy hand-stitched image of an old, disused quarry on the formal arrangement of tiles, surrounded by a patterned border. In the sketch above, both tiles and quarry are ancient and incomplete, broken by time and weather but still grand memorials to the passage of time. This idea could be constructed in separate units and then placed together as tiles are, on a large background of wall. Maybe some of the actual colour of tiles could show through here and there, for a ghostly effect.

Below:
Quarry Tiles

The Alchemist Project
by Penny Burnfield

For her Part II City and Guilds Embroidery examination, English embroiderer Penny Burnfield worked a series of pieces on the theme of Alchemy, the ancient forerunner of Chemistry whereby men sought to turn base metals into gold. Under the guidance of her tutor, Valerie Campbell-Harding, Penny constructed a number of items to symbolize articles which would have been used by the alchemists. These include a series of books containing writing on alchemy from different times and places, three vessels in which the transmutations appear to take place, and the robes, all bearing appropriate mystical symbols.

This is what Penny herself says about the subject: 'For nearly two thousand years, the world of science was dominated by Alchemy, a strange mixture of experimentation and mysticism. At its simplest level, it had three aims. First,

**Alchemist's Vessels,
by Penny Burnfield**
50 x 40 cm (20 x 16 in)
Machine embroidery
on various fabrics and
handmade paper
*Photograph by
Penny Burnfield*

the transmutation of base substances into gold by the use of the Philosopher's Stone. Second, to search for the Elixir of Life, and third, to search for the Panacea of all Ills. Throughout my own investigations, I have been intrigued by the mysterious and beautiful alchemists' symbols which were used as a secret code. I have also been amused by the fact that embroidery today is so much concerned with the use of false gold.'

Alchemist's Vessels (left) was worked mainly in machine embroidery on a variety of fabrics and handmade paper. Each vessel is richly beaded inside. The vessel on the right represents the transmutation of iron into copper. The central one transmutes silver into gold, and the one on the left, copper into silver. Each vessel is three-sided and has a different set of symbols on each face, but the spiral is used on all three as well as in the construction of the vessels as a universal symbol of life, growth, development and mystery. The photograph opposite (top right) shows the *Alchemist's Silver Vessel*, inside view.

The *Alchemist's Book* (opposite, bottom) was constructed in four linked sections and made to fold (see detail on page 115). The *Alchemist's Robes* (opposite, top left) were created for the character Subtle in Ben Johnson's play *The Alchemist* (1610). This photograph gives one a good idea of the scale of the vessels. The model for the alchemist was Penny's husband.

Far left:
Alchemist's Robes,
by Penny Burnfield
Appliqué, machine
embroidery and sequins
Photograph by
Penny Burnfield

Left:
Alchemist's Silver Vessel,
by Penny Burnfield
Inside view
Photograph by
Penny Burnfield

Below:
Alchemist's Book,
by Penny Burnfield
72 x 29 cm (28 x 11 in)
Goldwork and appliqué
Photograph by
Penny Burnfield

Ideas for Constructions

Constructions like Penny Burnfield's *Alchemist's Book* (see page 55) may at first seem complex but they are really no more than several pieces of the same shape and size fixed together. Arrangements such as this give more scope to include related bits of information, symbols and motifs in a unified way without their encroaching on to the same space.

The triptych is a similar arrangement with the extra advantage of 'compartments' behind the first layer. Many different formats can be found for this type of construction. The diagram shown opposite shows the format used by the artist Fra Angelico (c. 1400–1455) with a possible ten areas for the parts of the design. The two halves of the front cover (nine and ten) may join to show one complete scene. More simply, the format to the right of this shows ten larger divisions, though seven and eight, nine and ten may join to become one. This idea can be used for a folding screen composed of upper and lower sections which may or may not show a connecting design. The triptych may also suggest a door, transparent or otherwise, the outer view suggesting one thing while the inside shows something else. Many ideas could be expressed like this (see the section on 'looking through' on page 106).

Two other ideas on this theme are concerned with the folding aspect of parts, though paradoxically there is something equally attractive about these 'ground plans' before they are made up into three-dimensional pieces. Have you ever thought how embroiderable those books of printed box-shapes are, all ready to cut out and →

fold up into gift-boxes? Sheets of buildings for model-makers and children are far too attractive to assemble; they are much prettier left flat and decorative. In this state, ready but not made up, they seem to express a state of 'almost preparedness' without the ultimate element necessary to make them real, rather like a longed-for wish which has not yet materialized. I have often wanted to embroider a page looking like one of these unmade models, a pattern-page at odd angles complete with instructions.

The cube lends itself to this idea too, particularly if the design is arranged so that it flows from one side, across the fold, and on to the others. To check that the six-sided but flowing design will actually connect where it's supposed to, the cube should be made up in thin card first and stuck with glue or sticky-tape. The same can be done with a pyramid. Look at the following ideas based on boxes (plenty of punning words and fantasy suggestions) and three-sided figures. (See also Chapter Seven on Symbolism for more meanings to do with numbers.)

Shapely Words

Many words and phrases contain concepts of shape on which to base a design. As always, look out for the double meanings:

The square: square dance; meal; root; deal; squaring the circle; squaring up; set-square; T-square; public square.
The triangle: eternal triangle; tripod; trefoil; triptych; trilogy; trinity; third person (singular); three-cornered hat; trio; hat-trick.

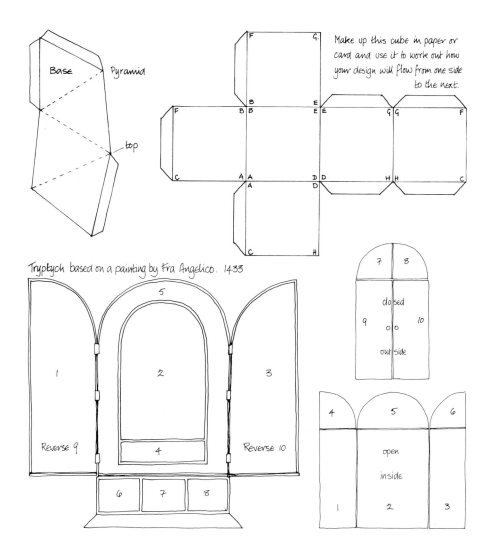

Base   Pyramid
top

Make up this cube in paper or card and use it to work out how your design will flow from one side to the next.

Tryptych based on a painting by Fra Angelico. 1433

Doubles: dual; duel; duo; Gemini; twins; dual personality; two-faced/head-ed; double-figures; double-barrelled; two-fold; deuce; doppelganger; double-cross.

The circle: to come full circle; loop-hole; smoke ring; roundabout; ring of fire; family circle; round table; encompass; squaring the circle; magic circle; wedding ring; stone circle; bull ring; ring road.

Pattern: patterns of behaviour; zig-zag; labyrinth; maze; network; lattice; grid; bio-rhythms; blueprint; borderline (case).

Scale: timescale; reduce to scale; chromatic scale; major/minor scale.

The cross: double cross; cross-dressing; cross purposes; crossbow; crossed lines/wires; level crossing; cross country; cut on the cross; crossed swords; cross-grained; crossed legs; crossroads.

The spiral: social whirl; revolution; whirlpool; helter-skelter; whorl; helix; pirouette; in a spin; spinning wheel; spinning top.

Boxes: box kite; box room; Boxing Day; chocolate box; ice box; gear box; sewing box; music box; wig box; flower box; voice box; pill box; boxing ring; window box; money box; box office; glove box.

Triptych
by Claire Johnson

This unusual and fascinating arrangement consists of a three-sectioned painted panel clearly linked by the richly-patterned borders and rollicking fish motifs. Claire's love of pattern and her subtle sense of humour shine through this piece, hinting at the multi-layered element which is an integral part of her work.

Triptych,
by Claire Johnson
30 x 20 cm (12 x 8 in)
Photograph by
Claire Johnson

Fragment Hanging
by Claire Johnson

The similarity between this machine-embroidered, slightly quilted piece and *Triptych* is obvious: the sections, the colours, the detailed patterns, the ragged edges. Another unusual construction, this typifies the artist's interest in the elements of surprise and investigation where sections overlap, tempting one to lift and explore. 'This', says Claire, 'appeals to our natural curiosity, while the quilted and padded techniques symbolize the human need for warmth, protection, reassurance and security'.

Fragment Hanging,
by Claire Johnson
30 x 30 cm (12 x 12 in)
Photograph by Claire Johnson

Mask of a Tree Spirit
by Molly Verity

Molly created this mask by pasting scraps of fabrics and paper on to spray-dyed and printed calico in a limited colour-scheme of greens, black and silver, on a base of chicken wire, clay Das and papier mâché. Machine embroidery was used to create much of the texture, while the addition of silver threads gives a sparkle of dampness. Tissue paper helps to create a wrinkled appearance, and many of the free-form leaves which appear on the branches are supported by wire. The inside of the mask is lined with pads of tissue paper.

Molly says this about her reasons for making the mask: 'I had been drawing and thinking about trees for some time, trying to find ways of expressing the spirit of them, especially oaks. This seemed to be easier to discover in Winter, when trees have a special appeal. Leafless, against a pale winter sky, encrusted with deep green moss and ivy leaves in a woodland undergrowth, a tree's personality is more apparent to the human observer. In all my work, I try to reflect some of the mystery in creation.'

Mask of a Tree Spirit,
by Molly Verity
92 x 46 cm (36 x 18 in)
Machine embroidery on
paper, fabric and calico

Narrative Embroideries

Some of the earliest known embroideries were made to record events of great significance in the daily lives of the people of the time, and to adorn the walls of a hall, palace or solar. These large wall-hangings were usually the work of several people, often working as a team in a workshop under the guidance of a professional designer. The ones which remain are no mean feats of artistry, if only for the way in which the vast amount of information has been made to fit into a limited space.

In the hangings of antiquity various techniques were used, including quilting, couching, close stitchery and appliqué. Formats are even more varied, and the amount of information packed into them is staggering. Most embroiderers will be familiar with the famous *Bayeux Tapestry*. Its long narrow format moves the eye onwards into the story with vigour and pace. Similar embroidered stories of battles and scenes from legends are known to have decorated the dwellings of royalty and wealthy nobility, in the same way that woven tapestries were used to make bare castle walls less chilling.

The *Creation Hanging*, located in Gerona Cathedral, Spain, dates from around 1100. Embroidered in wool on linen, it shows the labours of the months in compartments surrounding scenes of the creation inside a central roundel. In the corner spaces are figures of the four winds; the sun and year are portrayed figuratively and the centre shows Christ in the act of blessing. Explanatory words are scattered around the scenes and the circular borders contain more formal lettering for those who could read in those relatively illiterate times. The detailed activity must have filled the devout with awe and admiration.

The *Easter Hanging* from Luene Convent in Germany dates from around 1504. In wool embroidery on linen, it was commissioned by the Abbess Sophie von Bodendike in 1504. It is now in the Museum für Kunst und Gewerbe, in Hamburg. The brilliant colours and lively design celebrate the resurrection in all its glory, with angels, stars, bells, moon, animals and words in great profusion. In both of these embroideries, the dominant circle is used to symbolize the world and life. This would have been obvious to everyone who looked on these pieces hundreds of years ago, just as it is to us today.

Narrative embroidery is a popular method of recording and celebrating the doings of organizations, cities and countries, but it is not only national or world events that are worthy of depiction in this way. Narrative embroideries can also be planned on a smaller scale to record the activities of one person or family, or of the events within a group. A look at the ways in which some narrative embroideries have been made may suggest ideas for formats depicting both major and minor events.

At this point, I must mention three very famous narrative hangings that have been a source of inspiration to embroiderers over the centuries.

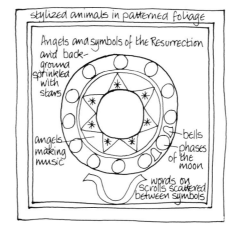

Left:
Sketch of the Easter Hanging, Luene Convent, Germany, c. 1504
475 x 420 cm
(187 x 165 in)

Below:
Sketch of the Creation Hanging, Gerona Cathedral, Spain, c. 1100

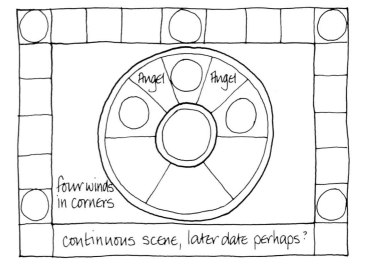

The Bayeux Tapestry (c. 1076–1086)

Although the *Bayeux Tapestry* is now in Bayeux, France, it was
actually made in England in 1066, to celebrate the victory of Duke
William of Normandy over King Harold of England in the Battle
of Hastings. The story continues from left to right along its entire
length, though some of the story is missing from the end. The
episodes are punctuated by decorative trees and sometimes
buildings. A narrow band above and below the main scenes contains extra information, legendary material, animals, mythological
beasts and birds and personal comments. Latin inscriptions are
inserted above and between the main action giving exact references to people, places and events. The *Bayeux Tapestry* was
couched in wool on linen, with outlining stitches, and measures
70.4 x 0.5 m (232 x 0.5 ft).

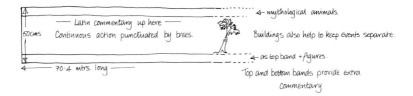

The Tristram Legend (c. 1300)

Worked in wool stitchery on linen in blue, red, yellow, green and
neutral, this large German hanging tells one of the stories of
Tristram in twenty-three scenes, punctuated by buildings. The
bands containing the story are placed one above the other
between more narrow bands of shields bearing arms of noble
families. The commentary runs in narrow bands above and below
the scenes. It is now housed in the Convent of Wienhausen,
Germany. It measures 404 x 223 cm (159 x 88 in).

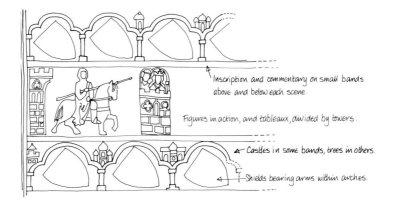

Border of flowers

Eleven of these shapes are used as containers for a series of events depicting earthly love. Begins and ends with monogram and arms.

The Malterer Hanging (1310–20)

This long, narrow hanging of the Upper Rhine (above) was worked in irregular close couching with stem stitch outlines in wool on linen. It was given by the Malterer family to the Convent of St. Catherine at Freiburg in Breisgau where their daughter Anna was a nun. It contains eleven quatrefoils, inside which are depicted scenes of earthly love. No commentary is contained here, though the scenes are recognizable and include some from classical literature. They are appealing in their direct-ness in describing the difficulties which the temptations of the flesh could lead to. The hanging is bordered by stylized foliage. It now resides in Freiburg at the Augustinermuseum.

The drawing below shows one of the quatrefoils from the *Malterer Hanging*. The meaning of the story is made quite clear through symbolism and body language. The young knight (symbol and shield), bends partly towards the queen (crown and raised throne) and partly towards the young lady to show the ring, (symbol of unity, love and marriage). The queen's head, tilted downwards, registers suspicion and displeasure, and her hands in a praying attitude suggest the message, 'May heaven preserve me!' The angle of the young lady's chin suggests defiance, but this may be reading too much into it. Her left hand and arm are definitely supporting and encouraging.

A quatrefoil from the Malterer Hanging, Upper Rhine, 1310–1320

The Warwick Panel

The *Warwick Panel* is composed of one hundred and thirty-three separate 18 cm (7 in) squares. The fifteen making up the central design were worked by members of the East Surrey Branch of the Embroiderers' Guild, and the remaining one hundred and eighteen by members of one hundred and four local organizations. The purpose of the central design was to show a selection of local buildings of architectural interest and local landmarks, while the symbolic squares represent organizations including the Mothers' Union, the Samaritans, Age Concern, Youth Clubs, The National Trust and the Women's Institute, among many others.

Work on the panel began with discussions in August 1985 after an appeal at a local Arts Council meeting. Once the idea for the panel had taken shape, design co-ordinator Liz Ashurst sent advertisements to newspapers and the local Arts Council Newsletter and to one hundred voluntary organizations in the area, inviting them to design and embroider a square to symbolize their activities. Funding was thought out at the beginning, to decide whether sponsorship for the project should come from individuals, local businesses or the local council. As ideas and designs were received, eleven group leaders from the local Embroiderers' Guild supervised, encouraged and supported over one hundred and four representatives of the organisations. In Liz Ashurst's own words: 'Our intention was to provide something creative which was a positive expression of community and would bring pleasure and harmony to the environment. We had complete novices rise to the challenge of design and method and it was a truly a community project with people meeting neighbours and representatives of other groups with whom they might not normally have communicated.'

Regarding the organization of such a huge project, Liz says: 'Organization at the planning stage is very important. You need an administrator to contact everyone and deal with the paperwork, a treasurer to keep the finances going and someone to handle the publicity, as well as a suitable place to meet and introduce the project to the participants. The co-ordinator needs good design expertise, and the surroundings in which the piece will be placed must be considered. The group leaders need not only strong technical skills but also the ability to pass on those skills and deal flexibly with people'.

Each design was approved before work began, and then colours were chosen to link with architectural features of the buildings and for their heraldic quality. Pure rainbow colours – yellow, orange, red, magenta, violet, indigo, turquoise and emerald – were co-ordinated by Guild members. The linen canvas used for the squares was 14 threads to the inch, and the threads used were a combination of matt crewel wools and shiny pearl cotton thread. Canvas embroidery was used throughout. Many different stitches were incorporated including tent stitch, chequer,

Hungarian, gobelin, rice and windmill stitch. The final arrangement of the squares was the responsibility of the design co-ordinator.

The fifteen central squares were embroidered by twelve members of the East Surrey Embroiderers' Guild in their own homes, with monthly meetings to ensure that stitches were being worked in the same direction over the same number of threads. Even after the work had been started, some unpicking had to be done after people's opinions about stitches had been considered. Anne Sillifant began by asking people what they regarded as the landmarks of the borough. It was important to combine historical aspects of the area with new developments. Over a period of months, working one whole day per week, Anne sorted and re-arranged hundreds of small sketches cut from card. She worked one row of buildings at a time, starting at the front. It was decided to use tones of grey, off-white and black to off-set the occasional jewel-like colours of vibrant green and scarlet highlights.

The next steps were to make an accurate full-size painting on card, with clear outlines, and then to trace off fifteen separate sections on to canvas squares, counting threads accurately so that each piece would register perfectly with its neighbour. A second tracing of each piece gave exact instructions about colour, stitch and thread, and each tracing was accompanied by a kit of threads. The central motif was completed in about six months, ready to be stretched, mounted, laced and assembled. By coincidence, the hurricane of October 1989 completely altered the tree-line of the area, so making the design something of an historical record. The complete project took about three years from start to finish.

The photograph on page 66, top shows the central portion of the panel. The photograph on page 66, bottom shows six of the logos from the *Warwick Panel* representing, from top left to right, Meadvale Women's Institute, Reigate District Riding Club, Women's Institute, Horley Tennis Club, Churchfelle Housing and Meals on Wheels.

The Warwick Panel
342 x 126 cm (11 x 4 ft)
Design co-ordinator:
Liz Ashurst.
Centre panel designer:
Anne Sillifant
*Photograph by
Keith Harding*

The Warwick Panel:
central panel
*Photograph by
Keith Harding*

Six logos from the
Warwick Panel
*Photograph by
Keith Harding*

The Quaker Tapestry

The *Quaker Tapestry* consists of seventy-five panels made to celebrate the spiritual insights which have motivated the Religious Society of Friends (The Quakers) since 1652. The purpose of the Design Co-ordinator, Anne Wynn-Wilson, was to create a craft project in which all members of the Friends could participate, whatever their age or ability and however far-flung their home in town or country. In working towards a corporate project, members were sure to make new friends and to discover more about the story of Quakerism.

The panels, originally set at fifty, eventually reached a total of seventy-five. Though seen as a unified whole, they were worked and mounted in separate pieces to make transportation easier and so that they could be worked on embroidery frames which were easily available to amateur workers. Like the *Bayeux Tapestry*, each design is divided into three horizontal sections and contains a written explanation. The designs were created by Anne Wynn-Wilson and a team of artists. Ann Castle and Ann Nichols taught the stitches and techniques used, often travelling across the world to supervise workshops and groups of embroiderers, skilled and unskilled. Well over two thousand people contributed their efforts in various ways.

Each panel measures 64 x 53 cm (25 x 21 in), and is worked on a specially handwoven wool which has a regular weave and a random stripe in the warp, giving guidance for horizontal and vertical lines of the design and the lettering. Thread colours were selected from

Sketch of Elizabeth Fry and the Patchwork Quilts, from the Quaker Tapestry

Appleton's crewel range to follow a restricted colour scheme for each panel, based on natural dye-types. Stitches and techniques were selected which would allow embroiderers of different ages and abilities to participate. Stem, split, knot and chain stitches were used throughout, and also Bayeux Point, as in the *Bayeux Tapestry* itself. For the lettering, a new stitch was invented by Anne which has been called Quaker Stitch; this is a combination of stem and split stitch.

The panel shown here represents Elizabeth Fry (1780–1845). In 1818, Elizabeth Fry persuaded the Governor of Newgate Prison to use closed hackney carriages instead of open carts for women prisoners about to be transported to Australia. As women in New South Wales were already familiar at that time with the technique of patchwork, every prisoner was provided with the materials and skills to make a patchwork quilt, including spectacles, if these were needed. On arrival at Botany Bay, the quilts could be used as proof of skill for those who were seeking work, or sold for a guinea at Rio de Janeiro. *Elizabeth Fry and the Patchwork Quilts* was taken in 1984 to Perth in Australia by Anne Castle who began work on it under a gum tree in a temperature of 104°. She was soon joined in the work by Friends in Adelaide, Melbourne, Hobart and Sydney, and the embroidery returned to England completed. The lower section of the panel was embroidered (and designed) by children in Australia and England. An exhibition of a number of the panels travels to various venues all over the world, while others are held permanently at Friends' Meeting Houses. The tapestry was begun in 1981 and took about nine years to complete.

The Hastings Embroidery

This embroidery was commissioned by the Borough of Hastings to celebrate the nine hundredth anniversary of the Battle of Hastings. It was worked by eighteen embroiderers from the Royal School of Needlework. The narrative begins with the Norman Conquest and ends in the Nineteenth Century. Each of the twenty-seven panels measures 276 x 92 cm (9 x 3 ft), though the scenes are meant to be viewed as one continuous whole. Worked in appliqué, the scenes are of different lengths according to the complexity of the material contained within them. While some overlap where the narrative runs from one episode into another, others are more clearly divided by arches and pillars. Dates and titles are given in small scrolls above the scenes. The drawing shows a detail from the Tudor period.

Sketch of detail from the Hastings Embroidery, the Tudor period

The Overlord Embroidery

A cross-channel invasion in the opposite direction is depicted in the Overlord Embroidery. It was commissioned by Lord Dulverton in 1968 from the Royal School of Needlework as a tribute to the effort made by the Allies during the 1939–45 war. It traces the planning and historical developments leading up to Operation Overlord, from 1940 until the invasion of Normandy and the Battle of Normandy in the same year.

The designs were the creation of Sandra Lawrence, taken from subjects chosen by a committee of service historians from the Ministry of Defence. Each of the thirty-four panels measures 2.5 x 1 m. In all, it measures 83 m long, 12.5 m longer than the *Bayeux Tapestry*. Fifty different kinds of fabrics were used on the background of linen on cotton, and the appliqué images overlap considerably where the scenes change, though some show more distinct dividing lines. It took twenty embroiderers five years to complete all the panels by 1973. It is now on permanent display at the headquarters of Whitbread and Co. Ltd., in Chiswell St, East London. The drawing shows a detail from the embroidery: *5th–6th June 1944*.

The Maldon Embroidery

This embroidery celebrates the one thousand years which have passed since the spectacular Battle of Maldon in 991. This Essex town on the estuary of the River Blackwater was the venue for a Norwegian Viking invasion led by Olaf Tryggvason who landed on the island of Northey. This was connected to the banks of the Blackwater at low tide by a narrow ford, and though the Saxon Byrhtnoth and his valiant men held the ford during a ferocious defence, the Viking forces were too strong. The Vikings won the Battle of Maldon and the fertile plains of Essex were theirs; the way to London was open.

In 1987, the Millennium Committee decided to commemorate the event with an embroidery depicting the life and character of the town during the years between 991 and 1991, starting with Saint Peter's on the Wall and Saint Cedd's cross, symbols of the arrival of Christianity in the locality. After the depiction of the battle, it was agreed that there should follow references to the most important personalities, activities, events, commercial enterprises, buildings, flora and fauna, up to the opening of the much-needed bypass.

The artist, Humphrey Spender, decided that, since the entire forty-two foot length was unlikely to be seen as an integrated whole, but rather viewed panel by panel, an overall grand composition was of less importance than a gradual development of the design. To avoid a disconnected appearance, horizontal gold lines at the top and bottom of the central section were introduced, and a subtle modulation

Detail from the Maldon Embroidery: panel 2
Photograph by Humphrey Spender

of tone and hue in the background was achieved by overlapping coloured nets. As with the Bayeux and Quaker embroideries, a narrow border above and below the central section provides space for extra information.

The artist's comments on his choice of colour are interesting: 'I decided that the general effect should be vivid, brilliant and rich in colour, limited only by the ranges of chosen materials. With the fabrics for appliqué, I found that this was quite a severe limitation in certain areas of the spectrum. I wished to avoid the realistic colourings of the greys, drab browns and blacks of weathered brick, colour-wash and concrete. Also, I wanted to give surprises in the difference between close and distant viewing. For instance, in the colouring of the houses, close viewing reveals thin stripes stitched with blue against yellow in close tones, blue against orange, or lime green against magenta, near complementary contrasts. But from a distance of about fifteen feet, these bright stripings mix optically to produce the comparatively neutral tints of weathered buildings. Black was virtually banned throughout. A thin stitched line of a dark hue, red, green, purple or blue, against a light background will appear to be black.

Each separate feature of the embroidery was analyzed both by the artist and the embroidery co-ordinator. Threads were listed and fabrics prepared for each piece so that these could be removed from the background and worked in the embroiderers' own homes. The final position of each feature was recorded with photocopies loosely attached to the background, which also allowed for last-minute alterations in placing and composition. The supporting fabric for the background was stretched over a wooden frame for each panel and the appropriate fabrics were stitched to this to receive the home-embroidered features. These features would then be stitched to the prepared background by the Thursday Ladies who gathered together once a week for this purpose. The complete set of panels took only three-and-a-half years from start to finish. At present it is temporarily housed in the Moot Hall, Maldon, Essex.

The photograph opposite (top) shows the beginning of the story. The combination of complementary colours blends to a lively grey stone tint when seen from a distance. The river Panta flows in the background. Part of the lower border, containing motifs of Saxon, Viking and Celtic influence, can be seen beneath the gold line.

The photograph opposite (bottom) shows a detail from panel two. It shows the body of Byrhtnoth being carried to Ely Cathedral, where his wife Aelflaed can be seen preparing an embroidery commemorating his virtues and deeds. The border shows local flora and fauna. The photograph on pages 70–71 shows Aelflaed with her embroidery in closer detail.

Right:
**Detail from the
Maldon Embroidery**
Designed by
Humphrey Spender;
embroidered by over eighty
ladies under the direction of
Lee Cash
Seven panels, each
182 x 66 cm (6 ft x 26 in)
*Photograph by
Humphrey Spender*

Below;
**Detail from the Maldon
Embroidery: panel 2**
*Photograph by
Humphrey Spender*

chapter four

The Human Form

On the face of it (another double-meaning!), it would seem that any design which represents and/or explores the way we feel, think or behave must necessarily involve some image of the human figure. It could be argued that the human figure is the outer wrapping of these complex processes. Word associations, as explained in Chapter One, may also demand that a human figure is included somewhere, even if one was not involved in the original meaning of the word or phrase.

If figure-drawing is a problem for you, there are ways round it, one of them being to practice – in a class, from a book, or just at home in private. Val Campbell-Harding's book, *Faces and Figures in Embroidery* (see Bibliography, on page 140) will also guide you through an amazing number of possibilities. However, there are two consolations to those who see figures in their mental scheme of things but are put off by the technicalities. One is that, as with all other design motifs, realism is not an essential ingredient. A look at some historic embroideries will show how quite primitive styles carry just as much vigour and meaning as more conventionally accurate styles; look at the *Bayeux Tapestry*, for instance, or the highly stylized figures found in many ethnic embroideries of more recent centuries. Many modern embroiderers, too, have often deliberately aimed for a spare, almost abstract, style in preference to realism. Any style is correct as long as it is appropriate and well-conceived. The detail from the *Guicciardini Quilt* demonstrates this point. It is believed to be Sicilian, dating from around 1400. Sometimes known as the *Tristan Quilt*, half of it is in the Victoria and Albert Museum, London, and the other part in the Museo Nazionale, Florence. Note that although the figure drawing is less than perfect, the attention to detail and the impression of violent action are indisputable.

The other consolation is that many ideas based on the human figure need not involve the actual figure at all but only a small part of it – a foot, a hand, or sometimes a garment. These can convey

Detail from the
Guicciardini Quilt
Sicilian, c. 1400

messages just as directly (or indirectly, if that is the artists' wish), as can the complete figure. In fact, one may derive the best of both worlds here by actually wearing the special garment and thereby adding the personal animation it requires. Think of a Birthday Suit, with the dates of birthdays embroidered all over it, being worn as a reminder at a family function! I have listed below various ideas to set your imagination running along this theme (figuratively speaking!). They are all phrases in common usage.

Interesting characters: Old Father Time; A Man for All Seasons; Jack Frost; May Queen; Green Man; Mother Earth; Four Elements; Five Graces.

Family matters: family ties (neck-ties?); group/gathering; tree; portraits; bond; circle; planning; extended family (using stretch-fabric?)

Words of a personal nature: personal charm; charisma; disposition; effects; details; identity; column. In person; first person singular; third person; displaced person; persona (grata, non grata).

Bodily functions: double figures; single figures; a figure of fun; public figure; figure of speech; body of opinion; busy-body; student body; bodyguard; body building; body language; able-bodied.

Parts of the body also give rise to many visual ideas. Think about the following word-associations to start with, and then dream up more of your own:

Head: room; rest; start; wind; gear; strong; turning heads.

Face: face up to things; on the face of it; typeface; multi-faceted; two-faced; about face; losing face; face-lift.

Arms: taking up arms; armed forces; arm's length; present arms; up in arms; lay down your arms.

Foot: stool; print; note; lights; hold; rest; stand on your own feet; swept off one's feet; feet of clay.

Other constructions make more interesting vehicles for figures than the more usual rectangle. Quilts are an obvious choice because of the three-dimensional qualities created, but raised work and sculptured pieces are also worth investigating. Check the following list for more ideas on this theme:

The mirror-image: *Would the gift the Good Lord give us, to see ourselves as others see us.* Well, this may not be possible, nor even desirable, but we can at least see our reflected images.

The bust: (as in statuary) perhaps with interchangeable heads, or two-sided faces, as with Janus, who could look both ways and thus see both the old and new years.

The totem-pole: could be a series of figures (fantastic or realistic) stacked in a vertical formation.

The Clock-face: grandfather/grandmother clocks, some with images of suns and moons, ships at sea, etc.

Portraits: family photographs or paintings. Old brown/sepia images of ancestors wearing bustles and looking severe.

Mask: this can be as brief or as concealing as you wish, realistic, imaginary, fantastic, horrific or humorous. Held on a stick by the wearer, tied on with ribbons, half-head, complete face or eyes-only (like spectacles). This is a large subject open to a huge variety of interpretations; masks have always and still can be used for many purposes. Few of us would deny having sometimes used a metaphorical mask to hide our true feelings.

Boxes are excellent vehicles for showing a personality in different guises. They have 'outer' and 'inner' parts, and you can incorporate lids and let-down sides, or drawers and compartments, rather like the stump-work boxes of the Eighteenth Century (see page 57 for some suggestions to set you thinking on this theme).

A wig stand, like the one used below, is another 'personal' construction. It could be used as the basis of a series of experiments to construct complete head-covers (including the face), in which you have one for each day; private or public image, good day or not-so-good.

Granny's Head
by Val Orr

Moulded on a wig-stand, this head (made life-size) epitomizes the ancient ancestor image of the sepia photograph dating back several generations, when white hair was tucked inside a frilled bonnet, indoors and out. The wrinkled face is covered by a network of needleweaving, and real spectacles rest on her nose.

Granny's Head,
by Val Orr

Moon and Water Carriers
by Belinda Downes

The idea stems from the influence of the Moon, her control over the tides and her affinity, as the feminine principle, with the water-carrying members of the zodiac, Pisces and Aquarius. Silver fish are seen in the water being poured out of the vessels.

Belinda writes with great clarity about her work and the reasons for her interest in statuary, its place within garden and landscape settings and the developments which took place around this theme: 'I was initially drawn to classical figures in gardens – Venus, Mercury and similar godlike beings, as well as those from the zodiac. Gradually, I began to show the character of each figure through the colour and mood of a piece, compositions which were carefully worked out with figures strategically placed to compliment one another. This playing with space and composition was important, creating a sense of distance by cutting off certain statues against the edge of the frame and having others at varying distances behind.

Preliminary sketch for Moon and Water Carriers, by Belinda Downes

'The mood was created, in many instances, by changing the time of day or night and sometimes by changing from night to day within the same piece. To add space and movement, I emulated the swirling brush-marks of painters by using dyed scraps of fabric.

'At first, my figures were often faceless, but as I needed to project their personalities more, facial expressions became necessary. Earliest ones took on expressions of indifference, my idea being that they had to; they couldn't change anything, they see all, but don't (or can't) take an active part. Perhaps I saw these creatures to be wise; to see so much through their hollow eyes and yet to say and do nothing. Then it occurred to me that this might be a tease – that as soon as our human gaze was temporarily elsewhere, they might move on their plinths, re-adjust their positions, or even climb down and race across the garden on to another plinth. Now magical and mysterious gardens began to grow, and the figures began to change, no longer classical but imaginary, with distorted shapes and angular faces. These were more playful beings, appearing to pass through the gardens with a purpose, carrying things. A friend suggested to me that perhaps I was capturing a moment, a particular time of day, night and place, always with the question, "What is that figure doing in that garden? Where is it about to go? What is it about to say?" I liked that interpretation, as I like the "keyhole" idea of peeping into another world on to something secret and mysterious.'

Moon and Water Carriers, by Belinda Downes
50 x 30 cm (20 x 12 in)
Padded figures on dyed muslin with straight stitches and satin stitch

Parisian Purse

This purse, made in Paris in around 1340, is made of linen and embroidered in silk in split, chain, stem and knot stitches. The background is couched in gold threads with red silk. The two sides depict lovers: on one side, a gallant well-dressed swain beckons to a reluctant maiden, but on the other, the maiden is obviously more eager than the lad. She grabs his hood and signals the direction they should go, and it is difficult to know whether he is horrified or merely shamming. In either case, the body language depicted by the designer is amusing and delightfully simple, the bag construction being a perfect vehicle for illustrating two sides of the same problem. A multi-sided purse would provide even more spaces for showing other facets of the story. My coloured pencil drawings were taken from photographs of the purse, which is in the Museum für Kunst und Gewerbe, Hamburg.

Right:
Purse, silk on linen
Paris, c. 1340

Far right:
Purse, silk on linen
Paris, c. 1340
(reverse side)

Misfits

This drawing is based on an appliqué wall-hanging that was designed around the idea of the children's game in which heads, bodies and legs are interchangeable, either on separate cards or in book form. The idea for this hanging, based on circus personalities, was sent to me by Angela Haigh who made it for part of her City and Guilds course. She called it *The Big Flop*, an amusing and ingenious play on words. She also embellished it with cords and ribbons hanging from the ends of the pole. Each section is made separately and fixed to the ones above and below by Velcro strips. In Angela's hanging, there are five characters, the fifth one being the Ring Master.

Right:
Misfits

Doll Figures

The method of transferring thoughts, feelings and ideas into the form of another body is as old as time itself. Human images have been a part of most societies since the dawn of history. Dolls made as toys for young children date back thousands of years. Nothing brings the past quite so up-to-date as seeing these ancient, often extremely ugly yet most-loved bundles of rag and bone.

Dolls made as companions for the dead are called grave dolls, and those made from the last cuttings of the harvest are known as corn dollies. Corn dollies represent the Earth Mother, the symbol of fertility – a necessary reminder of everyone's hope for regeneration during times when such things were not taken for granted. The whole history of doll-like images is rich with meaning, much of it connected to power, hope, well-being and the granting of wishes.

Dolls take on a wide variety of forms which can be exploited to good effect by embroiderers wishing to find an interesting vehicle for similar hopes, fears or wishes, as many of them have the potential to convey certain types of messages. The Jack-in-the-box elicits surprise, the shadow-puppet mystery and the glove-puppet eloquence. The upside-down doll plays a dual role, the string puppet requires someone else to make it come to life, and so on.

Here is a list of suggestions:

String-puppets (marionettes): allow manipulation, good for various postures, changeable, expressive, flexible.

Glove-puppets: easy to make, allows use of many embroidery techniques, manipulative.

Shadow-puppets: eerie, evocative, good for highly decorative outlines. Can be made in two dimensions instead of three, either over card, stringed or using sticks.

Stick-puppets: elegant but it takes some practice to make them appear natural. Indonesian and Javanese puppet-makers are known the world over for their skills in combining stick-puppets with shadow-puppets.

Upside-down doll: allows two characters to be built into one. A useful device for showing our alter-ego (see my *Upside-down Doll* on page 84).

Russian doll: stacking device; the sizes must be carefully worked out to make sure they fit together (see the illustration on page 85).

Back-to-back doll: flat or round, she has a different image on each side. Cube doll may be a four-sided figure. The old-fashioned dressing doll with hook-on clothes is a good idea too. Can be used to imply many changes.

Jumping Jack: really a string puppet, but usually flat.

Peg-doll: based on the old wooden peg, but could be soft.

Pedlar doll: carries a tray of wares. Highly detailed.

Jack-in-a-box: can be male or female, any type of figure.

Upside-down Doll: Autumn and Winter
by Jan Messent

The dual character of the figure represents both Autumn and Winter, the long skirts of one hiding the other. This last phrase seems a particularly apt way of describing what actually happens when the doll is turned upside-down.

The method of depicting two persons in one is useful as a demonstration aid for those who give lectures, but it has its limitations for exhibition purposes as there tends to be a 'do not touch' policy. However, it is open to a wide variety of transformations and the dolls are great fun to make.

The illustration opposite (top, right) shows an idea I had for a set of heads based on the Russian doll format, fitting inside each other to reveal or conceal a different generation. I would call it

Below, left:
**Upside-down Doll:
Autumn,
by Jan Messent**
41cm (16 in)

Below, right:
**Upside-down Doll:
Winter,
by Jan Messent**
41cm (16 in)

Ancestors. This idea could also be used to show a particular strain of family characteristics, different characters inside one person, different emotions or moods, or different people telling a family story. It could even be characters in the same story but with no blood relationship. The family of mothers and daughters planned in this drawing all show similar characteristics, as well as wearing the same brooch.

The printed sheet of card (below, right) from around 1900 has the pieces all ready for cutting out. When the limbs are connected, the puppets will be ready for play. Polichinelle is a hunchback holding a stringed instrument in his left hand. The bow is in his right hand. Perhaps a mistake was made in the printing of this version, but I note that the thigh sections are the same for both figures. This method of printing parts of figures on card or fabric within a rectangle has always been a source of fascination for me, for the pieces fit together so neatly that they seem to be more like biscuits in a box. An inventive development of this idea would be to arrange our own bodily bits and pieces like this inside a rectangle ready to be assembled. It could be titled, *Gone to Pieces* or *Pull Yourself Together*.

Top right:
Ancestors

Right:
a **Polichinelle and Arlequin, c. 1900**
  Printed board or fabric with figures in pieces
b **Upside-down figure**
c **Russian doll**
  The basis of several figures inside one

Jocelyn 1922.
Ethel. 1945
Sarah 1876
Elizabeth 1898

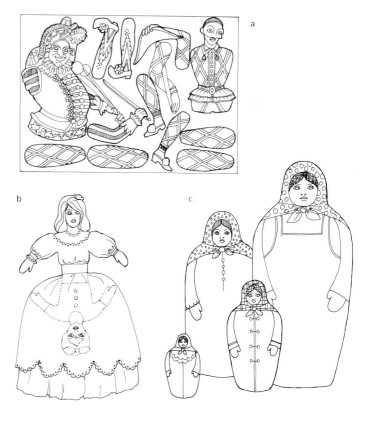

a

b   c

Objects of Obsession
by Mary Cozens-Walker

Mary Cozens-Walker is a professional artist whose painting career began at the Slade School of Art in London. She started to 'paint with stitches' in 1980 and took a postgraduate diploma at Goldsmith's College in embroidery/textiles. Her embroidery developed from two dimensions into three, and she began to use wood, metal, acrylic paint, yarns, sand, papier mâché, fabrics and threads to create images of the things she loved most. In the artist's own words, 'professional skills must be used to service the artist's intent; indulgence in techniques and craft skills should not become a refuge from creative thinking'.

Below left:
Forget-me-Not,
by Mary Cozens-Walker
84 x 44 x 32 cm
(33 x 17 ¹/₂ x 12 ¹/₂ in)
Mixed media
Photograph by Reeve
Photography
Setagaya Art Museum, Tokyo

Below right:
Detail of the top of
Forget-me-Not,
by Mary Cozens-Walker
99 x 105 x 5 cm
(30 x 41 x 2 in)
Photograph by Steve Orino

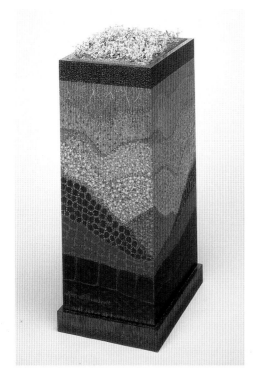

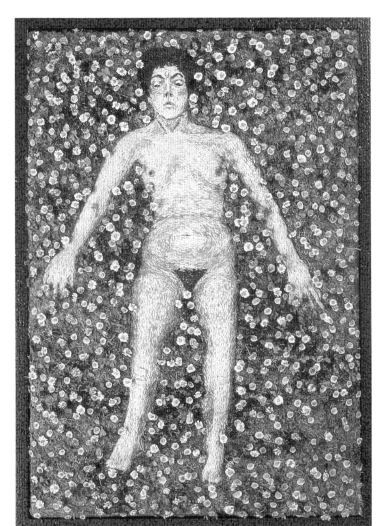

Much of Mary's work features her family and home, her objects of obsession. The two free-standing pieces, *Daisy Lawn* and *Forget-me-Not*, emerged as a direct result of seeing thirteenth-century tombs topped by recumbent effigies. *Forget-me-Not*, a delightfully amusing re-interpretation of the tiny blue flower, was a reminder of Mary's own garden in spring and of her desire to lie in the flowers as though part of the earth. *Daisy Lawn*, the first of the pair to be made, stems from a small patch of lawn encrusted with daisies which clicked on the feet and left toe-caps covered with yellow pollen. The pale figures against the green are reminiscent of the huge figures cut out of chalk down-land in the south of England. Below the figures, the strata are layered as though sectioned into a neat column by a mechanical digger, very much like the black-and-white line drawings in childhood encyclopedias.

Above left:
Daisy Lawn,
by Mary Cozens-Walker
84 x 44 x 32 cm
(33 x 17 ¹/₂ x 12 ¹/₂ in)
Mixed media
Photograph by Reeve Photography
Setagaya Art Museum, Tokyo

Above right:
Detail of the top of
Daisy Lawn, by Mary
Cozens-Walker
99 x 105 x 5 cm
(30 x 41 x 2 in)
Mixed media
Photograph by Steve Orino

Family Tree,
by Mary Cozens-Walker
105 x 99 x 5 cm
(41 x 39 x 2 in)
Photograph by Steve Orino

Family Tree reminds one, at first glance, of the ancient Green Man, the mythical Spirit of regeneration who can be seen in carvings and sculptures in churches and cathedrals all over Europe. It is particularly appropriate that Mary used six oak panels from a discarded organ at Highgate Congregational Church in London for her family tree with its quatrefoil windows, perfect for portraits. Outside Mary's London studio, chestnut trees provided the ideal type of foliage in which to part-conceal the faces of her loved ones and their family homes. Even her dog Rosie is portrayed in the piece.

The well-known structure of the family tree is given a very literal interpretation in this set of leafy panels.

Clothing

All human nature wears a mantle of grief.
Verdi's opera *Simone Boccanegra*

This particular aspect of the human figure offers an immense variety of possibilities to the embroiderer. These derive not only from the symbolism attached to garments and accessories, but also from the word-play which has developed and continues to develop on the subject.

Clothes may be all-revealing as a statement of one's personality, or all-concealing as a camouflage behind which one can disappear into the background. Their details can harbour secrets (in pockets or linings), or they can be removed from the figure altogether and be used as wall-hangings. Clothes can express the duality of one's nature; the reversible, inside-out aspect of a garment is useful for this.

As well as the clothes themselves, tassels, fringes and their embellishments can convey many extra meanings, depending on their placing, size and importance. Hoods, collars and other detachable parts can add to the complexity of a message built into the garment, as can fastenings which are a good indication of the era from which the garment is derived. For example, lacings evoke feelings of a feminine age when women were laced tightly into rigid hour-glasses, a skittish name (like leg o'mutton sleeves) which could be interpreted quite literally, just for fun.

Fox-fur
by Judith Smalley

Judith Smalley's *Fox-fur* illustrates the feelings evoked by seeing her mother wearing a dead creature around her neck. These are feelings that I remember well, too. I would sometimes creep upstairs to my mother's wardrobe just to stroke her fox-fur's nose and its tail, wondering if it minded hanging upside down in a dark cupboard. Like Judith, I was both fascinated and repelled by its glittering eyes and limply hanging legs. As Judith says, 'It seems incredible now that women in the 'thirties and 'forties should have considered it glamorous to drape dead animals around themselves'. Judith's fox is essentially vegetarian and environmentally friendly. He was made entirely from scraps of cloth and oddments of wool. His paws are velvet and although his legs hang limply, he has no claws.

Fox-fur,
by Judith Smalley
Photograph by Keith Hillyer

Kimono shapes are many and varied (see *Rainbow Kimono*, pages 40–41). They are not only all-enveloping, but also have sectioned panels which allow you to convey separate or connecting ideas on one piece. Made as a series, several kimonos could be read from one side to the other rather like a narrative or saga of events, developments or moods. Ethnic costume-patterns are particularly useful for their simple constructions and attractive fastenings, as well as their decoration, draping qualities and elegance.

Accessories are a rich source of symbolism, much of it dating back into prehistory and varying from country to country. 'Wearing different hats' is something women are familiar with in our changing roles – we are expected to be versatile in our abilities to be different things to different people.

All types of head-gear (whoops!) can be utilized to convey meanings: the hood for secrecy, the veil for mystery, the crown for glory, and so on. Gloves are steeped in meaning, as are umbrellas and parasols, fans (surprisingly female and thought-provoking items) and shoes. The custom of hiding a child's shoe in the foundations of a new building alludes to the belief that a child must be sacrificed as a protection against evil influences while the house exists. Children's shoes have, on occasion, been found concealed in walls and chimneys of very old houses, and shoes and boots are still tied to the cars of newly-weds to bring good luck. This last custom, however, also refers to the shoe as a

Below:
Kimono shapes

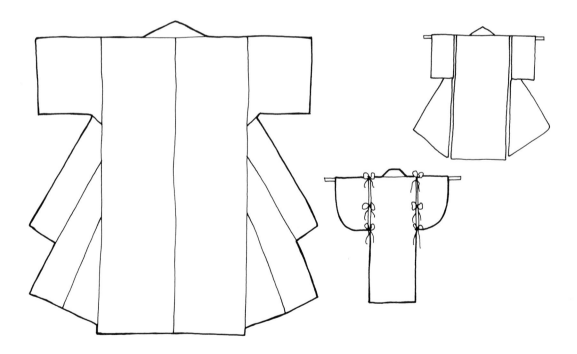

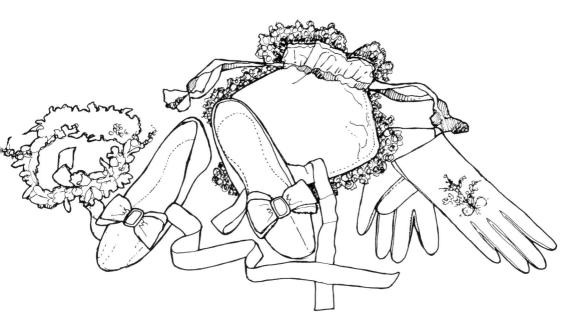

Wedding accessories,
mid-19th Century,
Manchester

symbol of the woman's submission to her husband as his property. Is that why Victorian women were so fond of presenting embroidered slippers to their husbands, I wonder?

Garments specially made for weddings are, of course, particularly symbolic, as are garments for other rites of passage, both for males and females. The decoration on garments for these purposes is particularly interesting, especially in those countries where embroidery on costume is an important part of a woman's life. The wedding accessories I have shown are from Platt Hall, Manchester, and were made in the mid-Nineteenth Century. They comprise white satin slippers with gold buckles and long ribbon ties, a white satin lace-edged drawstring purse, white kid embroidered gloves and a delicate wreath of wax orange-blossoms for the bride's head.

A look in any thesaurus under the headings 'investment', 'dressing', 'covering', 'clothes', etc. will provide an almost endless list of ideas on the subject of costume. Begin to collect phrases and quotations about clothes, and cut out pictures of fantastic and imaginative garments to boost your own creativity. I have started you off with some words and phrases that sprung to my mind on this subject:

A wolf in sheep's clothing; night gown (covered with stars and moons, perhaps?); night cap; capsize; life jacket; bedclothes; dust jacket; clothes horse; codpiece (this always provokes much hilarity among my students!); clothes line; law suit; clothes prop; salad dressing; hoodwink; wardrobe.

Alchemist's Hat
by Penny Burnfield

This embroidery is part of the set of robes for the *Alchemist Project* (see pages 54–55), using the spiral and the sun symbol on a vessel-shaped crown. The turban effect suggests the headdress of an Eastern magician. As with the creation of fantastic garments, hats need not necessarily be functional; they can remain purely ornamental as an expression of our love of dressing up, or of being someone else.

Alchemist's Hat,
by Penny Burnfield

Small Shoes,
by Claire Johnson

Small Shoes
by Claire Johnson

This pair of richly-encrusted, machine-embroidered shoes conveys a fairytale image. They could perhaps be part of a set of clothing for an enchanted person.

As all good fairytales tell us, clothes and accessories hold the power to transform us into something else, from bad to good (or vice-versa), from ordinary to interesting, from mortal to immortal, etc. The cloak which makes us disappear, the hat that gives us power, the shoes which give us speed or flight . . .

Campesina,
by Joan West
39.5 x 39.5 cm
(15 $\frac{1}{2}$ x 15 $\frac{1}{2}$ in)
Hand-stitched and appliqué
of tie-dyed cottons
*Photograph by
Joan West*

Campesina
by Joan West

Joan West's work illustrates her compassion for people caught
up in the desperate and seemingly hopeless struggle for survival,
whether through famine or political oppression. Her series of
embroideries based on the famines in Africa and on human rights
in Latin America combine the abstract and representational, the
realistic and symbolic, and are full of exceptionally strong imagery
as well as subtle metaphor. Colour, and the lack of it, is important.

Famine in Africa,
by Joan West
102 x 41 cm (40 x 16 in)
Fabric, paper and
stitchery
*The Embroiderers' Guild's
collection*

Texture is vital. Clichés are to be avoided, honesty sought at all costs. Joan's extensive research into these tragic subjects indicates her depth of feeling. Influences stem from television reports, newspaper articles and photographs. Exhibitions of ancient artefacts bring the past into the modern world with startling clarity. Amongst the symbolic decoration on Paracas mantles, the tragic narrative on Greek pottery and the complex patterns of bandages on Egyptian mummies, Joan finds links with her own ideas. By the same token, the media she chooses to interpret these ideas represent the same sources from which they come: old blankets and rugs, newspaper and cardboard boxes, handmade paper, scuffed suede and string.

Particularly striking is the haunted, mosaic-like face of the *campesina* (peasant) locked in the struggle against political oppression (see page 93). The hot pinks, yellows and reds are the positive female colours that are reflected in the peasant embroideries of Guatemala. Mosaics are represented by stitchery.

In the detail from *Woman in Net* (right), Joan shows part of a woman's face embroidered below and over net. This has the dual effect of suggesting a mosaic, and of being something that traps as well as saves. Thus the figure is caught in the circumstances of her own life, for better or for worse.

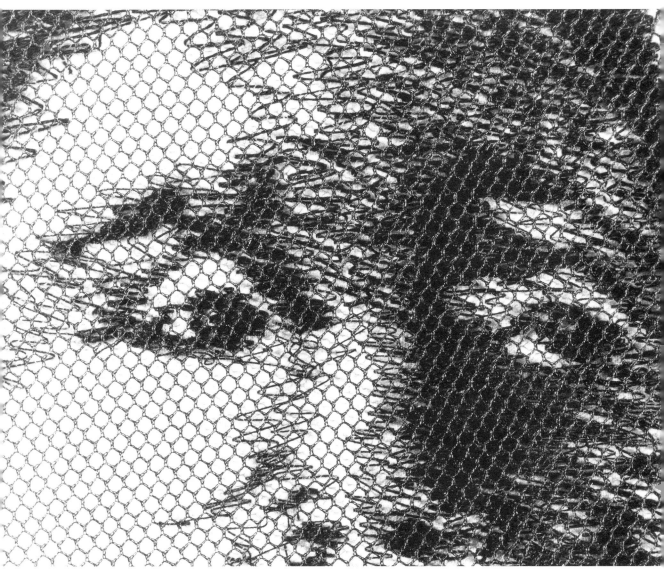

Detail from Woman in Net,
by Joan West
*Photograph by Doug Morley
Photography*

Music

It may appear at first glance to be well-nigh impossible to portray sounds in terms of visual designs, and from these into our own media of embroidery. The responses invoked by musical sounds are so deep inside us, inexplicable and elusive, that we can't even name them, much less give them substance. I would go even further and suggest that most of the time we can't even recognize them. Some music provokes such a multi-layered response – it may be both sad and happy, or expansive and intimate, or violent and gentle, at the same time. It may drag us through such a gamut of emotions within a relatively short space of time that we are left almost dizzy and breathless, unable to say what it was we heard that moved us so.

And yet, it may be easier to express what we feel about musical sounds through the media of fabric and thread than in words. The more you explore the connection, the more you will realize that it is indeed a similar language – although, paradoxically, it is words which highlight these links between the elements of music and the materials of embroidery. We have more links in our medium than painters, even, since we use tactile, textured things; threads, transparent fabrics and three-dimensional aids. These provide us with a richer vocabulary than almost anyone else.

It should be pointed out, however, that unless the piece of music being depicted is of very short duration, it is unlikely that a whole piece could be translated into embroidery in one go. A series, perhaps, but hardly one embroidery. To attempt this would be rather like trying to illustrate a complete story in one scene. It is much

more sensible to choose one particular part which you feel is easier and more straightforward to decipher, and to concentrate on this part alone until you have worked through its possibilities.

No investigation of this fascinating connection could ever be complete, and neither is there only one place to begin or end. Each embroiderer will operate on a purely personal level using his or her own favourite techniques, coupled with individual reactions to a particular piece of music. What follows, therefore, is a set of sub-headings introducing words common to both music and design (and embroidered textiles), with suggestions and comments for you to pick up and use as you wish. In looking at these lists, you will realize not only that we have many words in common, but that visual ideas and images can be evoked almost instantly at the sight of them. The words themselves become a stepping-stone, through which sounds can be translated into graphic concepts.

Pictorial Music

This is music which 'paints a picture', often titled in such a way that leaves the listener with no doubt about its intentions. Saint Saens' *Carnival of the Animals*, Mussorgsky's *Pictures at an Exhibition*, Vivaldi's *The Four Seasons* and Elgar's *Pomp and Circumstance Overture* are all obvious examples, and you can probably think of many more. Even more specific are operas, songs, ballets and musicals, which are nearly always directly 'about something'. Although this may appear to relate more to the stories than to the music itself, our translation of it need not be pictorial. In any case, if the words are in a foreign language then it is more likely to be the music that appeals to us rather than the actual meaning of the words. Our interpretation could be symbolic, abstract or impressionist, coloured by music as well as by events.

Consider tragedy, such as *Romeo and Juliet* – or ritual, such as *The Rite of Spring* – or magic, such as *The Magic Flute*. These are all full of symbolism and colour – a designer's field-day! Without getting too involved in the pictorial aspect, it is not too difficult to take any one of these titles and design a piece of embroidery using symbols, colours, patterns, motifs and textures to signify our reactions to the music on a personal level.

Musical Shape and Form

Many of the names given to music suggest images, shapes, concepts and patterns. These include:

Pastorale; fantasia; theme and variations; tone-poem; rhapsody; romance; fugue; composition; medley; hymn; prelude; movement; overture; suite; rhythm and blues; nocturne; chorus.

Most of these words describe forms, times of day, scenes, patterns and so on. It would not be difficult to elaborate on any of these ideas by listening to the appropriate piece of music and adding extra information by the use of colour and pattern.

Dance words are particularly appropriate; think of terms like 'gavotte', 'minuet', 'pavanne', 'square dance', 'foxtrot', etc. These have in-built patterns on which you could base a design. Astronomical dances were invented by the Egyptians and designed to represent the movements of the heavenly bodies. Dancing Water is a magic elixir common to many fairytales – it is said to restore beauty and youth.

Song words appear to divide themselves into certain numbers or groups, the colour and type of decoration depending on the age or location to which they belong. The exact reference will depend on the specific piece of music. For starters, try:

Aria; solo; duet; trio; quartet; plainsong; chant; chorale; madrigal; folk song.

Morris Dancers
by Anne Siess

Anne and her husband live in Canada and are keen morris dancers, often hosting visiting teams from England and paying return visits. She is a keen embroiderer.

I find in this piece the product of a particularly courageous mind, for whereas most of us would play safe and place the focal point (the white-robed morris men) towards the centre of the rectangle, Anne has chosen to place them up in the top right-hand corner, as though defying all the generally accepted rules. She leaves more than one-quarter of the space bare and places strong bands of contrasting tones right across the top half from side to side. And yet it works – why?

For one thing, the eye is dragged upwards (kicking and screaming?), through those fascinating reflected shapes of buildings on the lower left and towards the white band. Once there, the eye is then immediately caught by the upside-down reflections of the dancers whose legs overlap on to the darker bands above. We find ourselves so busy trying to work out the relationshp of these reflections to their shapes up on dry land that before we know it, we are examining the most interesting part (the reward, so to speak), before taking a cursory look at the grass and then back down into the reflections again. The red background behind the dancers is picked up in their red cross-bands and those of their reflections, though the latter have been overlaid with net to soften the effect.

A tiny square of green in the bottom right-hand corner forces us to look, defying us to ignore any part of the embroidery in case we should miss something.

From a musical point of view, I feel that as the viewer I am obliged to watch without hearing any of the sounds – the scrape of the fiddle, the breathless accordian, the jangle of the bells around the legs and the clacking of the sticks as they hit in the centre of the dance. I watch them group and re-group, throw their arms into the air, wave their kerchiefs and leap high into the air to the music inside my head. But I have the bonus of being able to see two sets of dancers for the price of one.

Morris Dancers,
by Anne Siess
61 x 25.5 cm (24 x 10 in)
Appliqué and hand
stitchery
Photograph by Anne Siess

Words of Pattern

Once you have decided upon the general form of the piece, these words of pattern, being very visual, will give further information about the sounds you are hoping to translate. Roll them around in your head to see what they might look like; they describe patterns, rhythms, shapes inside the framework, strengths and weaknesses. Think also about the words used for particular parts of music. Many of these can become key-words:

Repeat; counterpoint; scale; chromatic; arpeggio; chord; motif; key; quaver; accent; stave; bass.

These words can often be expressed in terms of blocks of shapes with ascending or descending lines, growing larger or smaller, louder or softer. Lines, under or over the main shapes, can imply other strands of sound – voices overlaid, other instruments and undercurrents of bass-lines or sustained chords. The weight of these (i.e. the lightness or depth of sound) can be indicated by the relevant heaviness of the line, from a heavy cord (or chord?) to a fine golden thread.

Think of shapes when you listen to music. Ask yourself to identify it in descriptive words, such as 'rounded', 'angular', 'broken', 'flowing', 'fast currents', 'spiky', 'hollow', or 'dark'. Next, try to be even more discerning and listen for further information. At this stage you might identify 'overtones of metallic sounds', 'beads of staccato sounds', or 'threads of broken velvet ribbon underneath'. Write these down as you listen to the same piece over and over again. You might find it helpful to make some sketches to clarify your thoughts.

Musical Colour

The colour of a piece of music is easier to see than its structure. The structure is often fleeting and difficult to pin down for long enough to analyze it. The colour, on the other hand, usually stays rather longer – at least for a part, if not the whole, of a movement – and for this reason it is clearer in our minds. It may sound strange to attach a colour to a piece of music, but it can be shown fairly simply that there is some degree of universal agreement on which colours match which sorts of music. I carried out an experiment to demonstrate the truth of this with a workshop of over twenty people. I asked them to tell me what colour they thought the *Sanctus* from Faure's *Requiem* was, after thay had heard it two or three times. They wrote their answer down on a piece of paper, and were not allowed to change their minds as the answer was given. About three-quarters of them described it as 'blue-grey', and the others gave good reasons for choosing 'opposite' colours to correspond to the contrasts in the change of key and strength of sound. It was not a matter of getting the answer 'right' or 'wrong'; what was interesting was that, by and large, we all felt the same way about the piece, some after hearing it for the first time.

Colour and tone are, of course, vital to both music and embroidery (see Chapter Two on page 34 for more on using colour).

Take the words used by musicians themselves to imply this extra dimension and see how you might apply the same words to your own design:

Harmony; discord; unison; light and shade; dominate and subordinate; tone; monotone; atonal; chromatic; counterpoint; con brio.

More general words can often apply to sounds as well – words like 'warm' and 'cool', 'metallic', 'vibrant', 'misty', 'strong', 'primary' and 'subdued'. If you stop to think for a moment, you will no doubt be able to find pieces of music in your memory which fit almost every one of these categories, either wholly or in part.

Musical keys tend to have definite colours, too. Generally speaking, major keys are represented by strong, clear, primary colours, while minor keys tend to be represented by softer and more subtle, subdued tones. This is directly linked to our own responses which identify the major keys with positive thoughts and the minor keys with more negative ones such as sadness, longing and unfulfilment.

Instrumental Sounds

This is more like a game than an exercise, although you will find it useful when you come to designing. Try to link the materials of embroidery (including different colours) to musical instruments. Do not limit yourself to those found in orchestras – mouth organs, accordians, tin whistles and pan-pipes can all be assigned a certain material.

For example, do you 'see' the sound of the clarinet as being velvety and soft? A rather rich plum colour? An elegant brocade, perhaps? Or a slub shot-silk of violet and green, with threads of antique gold? Or a trumpet – sparkling and clear, honey-coloured and transparent, glittering with gold threads and beads? Or a violin – more like a thread than a fabric, fine and taut but also strong and delicate. You might use criss-crossing, weaving, embroidering sounds of net or lace.

What about the piano, the bassoon, the piccolo, the cello, the tuba? What about the fabrics and colours of a brass band – the shapes; the gold braid; the primary, earthy rawness of it? Can you see it? Can you hear it? If you're smiling as you read this, it means you can!

Any thesaurus will give you dozens of words linked to sound, music and related words, but be aware of other sources that might spark off ideas along these lines. Such words can be found in advertising literature, in newspapers and on concert programmes. Here are some words and phrases to start you off:

Taking soundings; sounds good; faint sounds; whispers; soundtrack; fanfare; transmission; hearing-aid; high-fidelity; swan-song.

Take another look at Chapter One on Word Associations, to remind yourself of the double meanings to be found in almost everything. Try to think of the alternative meanings and title your work so the viewer has to think about what it means.

Paint sketch of Faure's *Sanctus*
by Jan Messent

The paint sketch shown overleaf represents the central passage in the *Sanctus* from Faure's *Requiem*. It is not an exact basis for an embroidery design – that would be softer, more flowing and less angular. The sketch merely attempts to show how sounds can be shown as patterns. It also demonstrates how one particularly interesting passage can be encapsulated, although it must be said that every person who hears it will 'see' it differently (and so, on another occasion, might I).

1   The diagram begins at the left with layers of rocking vocal sounds which change from a minor to a major key. This part of the music has had to be condensed in the diagram as it takes several minutes. The light green represents female voices, the darker green male voices.

2   The tent-like structure denotes the sound level reaching its loudest point in the centre and then tailing off. This shape is based on crescendo marks.

3   The heavy vertical bars, each one divided into five chords, are strongly pronounced by the orchestra while the male voices cut across them.

4   A trumpet sounds two sets of triplets, three times. These are shown as the yellow squares in the central area.

5   The sounds are at their loudest in the centre, hence the deeper tones. They fade away quickly after that when the female voices re-appear, underscored by soft male voices which pick up the rocking rhythm again.

6 Vertical lines suggest the stability of the rhythm, like scaffolding. Horizontal lines suggest movement through the structure, sustained vocal sounds on a repetition of three notes, shown by the pattern of diagonal lines as they might be seen on the score.

7 Finally, artistic licence allowed me to juggle with the shapes and lines to make them meet and dovetail in a way which balances and pleases the senses. Which is, after all, what the music does.

Paint sketch of Faure's
Sanctus

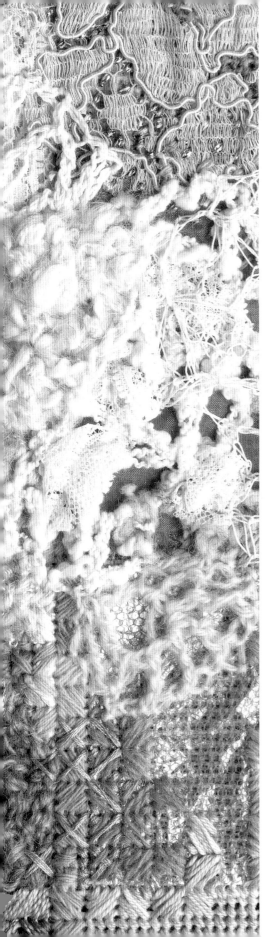

Sibelius
by Jan Messent

Modern music is less blatantly structured than that of earlier periods; its 'scaffolding' is better hidden than previously. We recognize its meaning on a different, more primitive level. Consequently, it is difficult to determine what we are hearing, and how that might be translated visually. What we are left with is more of an impression, similar to an impressionist painting where the elements are less well-defined and the resulting impression depends almost as much on the viewer's responses as on the painter.

A comparison of the paint sketch on page 103 and *Sibelius* may go some way towards explaining the different approach taken here. In this case, the vertical 'scaffolding' is represented by wide and narrow bands of 'sound' which overlap each other, are lost and then re-surface again. Across these flow diffused 'sounds' of colour which compact at some points and then thin out, allowing the underneath layers to show through (i.e. to be 'heard'). Hence my use of dense, highly-textured free-style knitting/crochet fabric which opens out into a lace-like effect, showing a structure beneath that is implied by the canvaswork.

Sibelius,
by Jan Messent
25.5 x 22.5 cm
(10 x 8 ³/₄ in)
Applied knitting, crochet and
fabrics to canvas,
with canvaswork
stitches

chapter six

Illusion

This short chapter suggests some of the ways we can use fabrics and techniques to present things differently from the usual head-on approach. It encourages you to see through things, shapes, structures and distortions, and to link these ideas to word associations and to your lines of thought.

First, take the concept of 'looking through'. This can be considered in two ways: firstly, think of looking through a framework to whatever is beyond. This will affect the shape of your design. Some suggestions are:

Windows – shop, house, greenhouse, office-block, etc.; door – wide open, ajar, cracks, keyhole; passageway; corridor; pillars; arches; ruins; banisters; fences; railings; scaffolding; bridges; wheels; goldfish bowls; chains; nets; grass; reeds; tree branches and roots.

Secondly, think about looking through things that obscure or alter your view. The 'looking through' things on this second list will affect the image rather than the shape of your design:

Glass – frosted, patterned, coloured; mist; haze; smoke; fog (mists of time); water; aquarium; waterfall; rain; mirror; prism; crystal ball; magnifying glass; telescope; binoculars; net curtains; transparent fabrics; spectacles (possibly rose-coloured?); drinking glass; kaleidoscope; zoom lens.

In different ways, we speak of 'looking through' the eyes of; 'looking through' letters, drawers, books and clothes; 'looking into' the past and future; 'looking into' a problem; 'looking ahead'; and 'looking good'. As you did in the first chapter, apply a literal interpretation to these colloquialisms and see how you can twist them round to give them both a metaphorical and a literal meaning. Don't forget that ideas can be combined, but not too many in one go!

Some fabrics are transparent or opaque and some embroidery techniques can be made to appear so. Here are some suggestions for materials that may help to add meaning to any of the foregoing ideas: net (curtains), handmade nets (e.g. macramé, fishing), scrim, organdie, chiffon, knitting, crochet, needleweaving, lace, drawn and pulled-thread work, canvaswork (left bare), cutwork.

Moving on to other illusory ideas, we could again revert to the first chapter on word associations to make a list of everyday words which also apply to our use of fabrics in embroidery – words such as 'distort', or 'distortion' (of the truth?). Some more examples are listed overleaf.

Private View,
by Kay Greenlees
82 x 52 cm
(32 x 20 ¹/₂ in)
Appliqué, paint and machine
embroidery
Photograph
by Kay Greenlees
Alan and Viv Goddard's
collection

Withdraw (threads, ourselves); displace (threads, persons); manipulate (people, events); fold (to enfold); soft; smooth; regular/irregular (pleats, actions); abrasive, prickly (people); graduate (layers); fold and twist; fray (tempers); tortured (minds, thoughts); padded; pleated (depleted); burnt and tattered.

A look at the structure of fabrics will also point out some areas where extra weight can be added to a message within your design. There are many examples of embroideries in this book which illustrate how the choice of materials is highly significant in conveying information about the subject.

a Fabrics with obvious structural patterns include canvas, rug canvas, twill, binca, all counted threads, nets, corduroy, knitting, crochet, cellular, hessian and scrim, seersucker and quilted fabrics.

b Fabrics with soft, furry textures include velvet, loop and pile fabrics, felt, lint, fleecy wools and tweeds, knitting, crochet and fake fur.

c Fabrics with smooth, fine textures include organdie, organza, silks and satins, calico and lawn, plastic, leathers and papers.

d Double-duty fabrics: inasmuch as all fabrics have two sides, two directions, etc., some are more useful than others. These include velvets and corduroys, reversible prints, brocades, woven-in patterns, shot silks and dupions. Link these materials to ideas which depict duality or two-sidedness, for example: double-take; double-back; double and twist; double summertime; day in, day out; ups and downs; back-to-front; reversal; change your tune.

Techniques vary so widely in scale, overlapping each other in so many combinations, that it is virtually impossible to list them in a way which would indicate their usefulness for a particular purpose. Nevertheless, it is still possible to associate some techniques with particular images, just as Claire Johnson associates her padded sculptured pieces with man's longing for cosiness (see page 59). Patchwork, for instance, still has a homely image; small areas of faded patchwork and/or appliqué spell nostalgia, plain and wholesome living, the pioneer spirit and gas lamps. And in spite of having made every effort to update our use of stitchery, there are still plenty of us who remember our first lazy-daisy stitches, associating them with tablecloths too large for us to enjoy embroidering and tray-cloths which no-one ever used. There is no doubt that certain stitches hold memories for us. Why not make use of them once more?

Food for thought: what is 'the fabric of society'? And what is 'moral fibre'?

Creating Visual Illusions

Photographs can be used to combine ideas and to convey messages and feelings in an unusual way. One of the funniest cartoon drawings I ever saw was of a woman reflected in a mirror which showed the back of her head instead of her face. The front and back of her head were, apparently, both the same.

The figure in the doorway is composed of two photographs. The one in front is my husband at the front door returning home from work, and the one behind is a window in a Norwich church. One photograph superimposed on the other may give the impression of entering or leaving a cage (prison or safety), or of anticipation, or safe return, depending on the way the design is treated by the embroiderer.

Dreams are illusions which we tend to forget and re-bury in the light of day. Try to remember them, especially any recurring ones; they may be pointers to another piece of embroidery. Magic and superstition, also illusions, are regarded less than they used to be, as are fairytales, folklore and wonderful old wives' tales. But all of these can pave the way to more imaginative thinking. Conjurors, magicians, wizards . . . these are materials of illusion which were used in the past as an escape from ordinariness and predictability, or as an explanation for seemingly inexplicable happenings. Outmoded or not, they can take us into other realms, helping us search within ourselves and release feelings that have been locked away since infancy. Read a fairytale and see.

Visual illusions

Sketchbook Fragments
1992–93,
by Claire Johnson
22 x 15 cm (8 ¹/₂ x 6 in)

Sketchbook Fragments 1992–93
by Claire Johnson

Two pages from the sketchbook of the embroiderer Claire Johnson explain one of the preliminary stages in her designing process. She says: 'I work with a sketchbook, making daily observations through drawing and collage, tearing and rearranging pieces to make fragmented compositions through which bits of other pages can be seen. Thus the sketchbook is a visual experimental diary which provides information to develop into hangings, books, purses, shoes and watercolours'.

Claire admits to a love of pattern, both historical and contemporary, and says that the elements of humour, surprise and investigation have always been important to her. She encourages people to look at and investigate her work more closely, and to move sections of it to reveal other points of interest. This notion of lifting to explore the undersides, looking through gaps and spaces, tearing and rearranging pieces of pattern can be used to suggest the duality of things. Ideas, thoughts, hidden meanings, darker and lighter sides can all lie behind apparently simple exteriors. This approach can also be used as a way of showing that things are not always what they seem to be.

Mirror Frame
by Marjorie Halford

Inspired by the beautiful borders that surround the Mughal paintings of India, this delicate mirror frame was hand-embroidered mostly on Indian fabrics, using Indian threads (except for the gold).

Mirror words and phrases include: magic mirror; hold a mirror up to nature; seen in a glass darkly; reflector; hand-glass; looking into things; exposed to view; before my eyes; all will be revealed; eye-witness; sight-seer; show your face; framed; point of view; private view; exposure (indecent?); peep show; lookalike; on the face of it; behind the scenes.

Reflect on it!

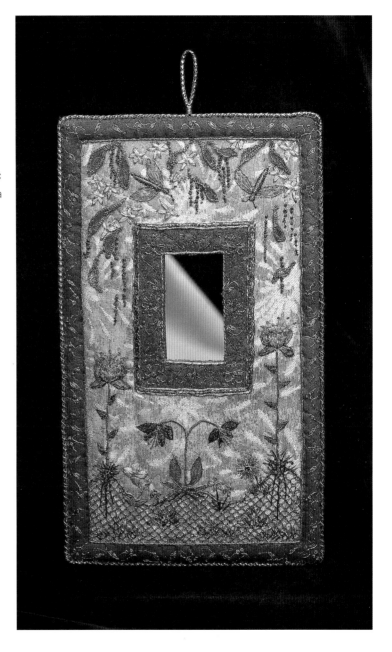

Mirror Frame,
by Marjorie Halford
23 x 13 cm (9 x 5 in)

chapter seven

Symbolism

To embroiderers, symbols are probably the most important and readily-available design elements through which to express abstract thoughts, ideas, feelings, emotions and personal statements. The first decision to make is whether to use well-known traditional symbols that will be easily understood by most people, or personal symbols which are meaningful only to yourself and which others will only be able to guess at unless you choose to explain them.

This choice can be helped by understanding the categories into which symbols fall – not subject categories (animals, flowers and so on), but more basic ones. Before we became a literate nation, symbolism was the main method of recognizing information. Shops and ale-houses had only pictorial signs above them; church walls were lavishly decorated with vivid scenes of life and death; paintings, jewellery and embroidered items held symbolic messages every bit as clear as written ones. Everyone knew the significance of the symbols as if his life depended upon it, which indeed it sometimes did.

Nowadays, we are less dependent upon such recognition, and yet it takes only a little practice to set these aids once more into motion and to discover analogies between things, animate or inanimate, which will help us to express our ideas in embroidery. The world around us abounds with symbols for indefinable but real meanings.

Lines and shapes, for instance, can convey meanings simply by their structure. They can strongly suggest behavioural patterns corresponding to mood or bodily posture. Leaning, rhythmic, rocking, prickly, graceful lines; horizontal, vertical, diagonal or multi-angled shapes will all convey a certain feeling. For more suggestions along these lines, see my drawing 'Lines and Moods' (opposite).

The inner responses provoked by lines and shapes are part of a larger and more complex area of symbolism known as 'archetypal' in which personal images within the individual are given particular attributes, qualities or powers. Archetypes are personal, although some are adopted via our religion, our upbringing, and our social traditions and rituals.

A much-used form of symbolism is personification. This relies on finding a character which will personify a specific thought, mood or ideal. It stems from the history of ritual and theatrical performance where people dressed up to represent such things as Truth, Beauty and Courage. This was a particularly favourite entertainment at the court of the Tudor monarchs, where courtiers had to guess the identity of the attribute before them.

Chinese painters were historically particularly gifted at portraying abstract thought by means of the human form, not merely by the expression on the face but also by the lines, shapes and colours used to provoke an appropriate response in the viewer. This technique has been employed by many artists in other cultures, especially in modern art, where fractured shapes and discordant colours leave one in no doubt of the emotions behind the imagery.

Some symbols, called 'actual object' symbols, are successful because they have direct associations with what they represent. For example, the sun represents daylight and warmth, and the moon represents night-time, darkness and mystery. The rose represents the heart's blood, and the pomegranate (because it is so full of seeds) represents fertility.

Imaginary symbols relate to 'unreal' things: fantastic animals, demons and dragons which exist only in our minds. Traditionally, these are made to represent real emotions that we struggle to control, such as anger, fear, greed, strength and so on. Such symbols are often steeped in folklore and tradition, and they are so familiar to us that it would be almost impossible to replace them with new ones.

Joint symbols are combinations of two or more related (or totally unrelated) objects which give an extra meaning to a message. For instance, a face inside the sun or moon will show whether it is male or female. A heart surrounded by flames, arrows or flowers will explain the emotional state of the lover who sent it.

The subject matter of symbolism is immense, not only within one culture but

Lines and Moods

a nervous, agitated, unsure, panicky, uncomfortable, anxious, highly-strung, jumpy, excitable

b regular, reliable, predictable, even, monotonous

c fractured, unsettled, conflicting, directionless, difficult, confrontation, friction, strife, discord, interference, disagreement

d disconnected, shattered, incoherent, insecure

e fast-moving, hurried, turbulent, fierce, boisterous, stormy, rough, wild

f smooth, calm, easy, stead, strong, continuous, lilting, even, fluent, unruffled

g bouncy, springy, light-hearted, progressive, buoyant, confident

h halting, unsure, doubting, troubled, apprehensive, tense, hesitant

113

across the world where meanings differ enormously on almost every item. Not only that, but time has also changed the meanings of things; some are so out-of-date that their meanings now hold no significance for us. Still, even this aspect is intriguing – we may find something worthy of revival that has a particular application to our own state. Who knows?

Numbers play an important role in almost every aspect of our daily lives. House numbers, birthdays, time, dates, accounts, recipes and measurements are just some of the numbers we continually use. Not surprisingly, numbers have always held an important place in symbolism, and if the idea of using them appeals to you, consider the following:

a Constructions with the relevant number of sides, facets, angles.
b Number rhymes.
c Your house numbers. (Amazingly, all five of my married homes have included the numbers one or two, or both.)
d Years of your life, or family years.
e A particular time, date, or year you wish to record.
f Limit your work to a certain number of colours or threads, or make it a certain size to correspond to your chosen number.

Terms of Expression

Symbol   something that represents or stands for something else, usually by convention or association, especially a material object used to express an abstract idea.

Attribute   property, quality or feature used to represent a person or a thing.

Allegory   story or picture with a parallel meaning in addition to the literal one; a description of something under the image of something else. Often the characters or scenes convey a deeper meaning than the original would suggest.

Metaphor   figure of speech (or, in this context, a designed image) that describes one thing in terms of another that is related to it by analogy, e.g. 'she's a lamb', meaning that the person is sweet and gentle.

Conceit   metaphorical image of a witty or far-fetched kind, used in past times as a form of flattery.

Simile   figure of speech (or design), that expresses the resemblance of one thing to another of a different category, usually introduced by 'as' or 'like', e.g. 'as clear as crystal', or 'the clouds were like cotton-wool'.

Significant numbers can be introduced into other symbols, such as the number of stars in a circle or points on a sun. They can be used in borders and sections, as sides to a shape, and so on (see my embroidery *Nocturne* on pages 120–121). Mathematical formulae can be expressed visually in various ways; you could combine multi-sided constructions, keep to a certain number of colours, or make the finished piece a certain size. You could use a certain number of strands in the thread, or insert the number of days it took to make. Alternatively, as with old samplers, you could embroider the dates on which you began and finished. These are all hidden messages, of course.

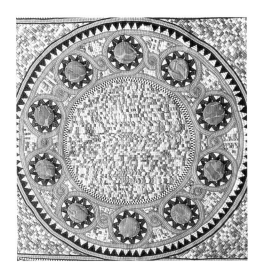

Left:
Mosaic Floor Quilt,
by Barbara Howell
228 x 228 cm
(90 x 90 in)
Appliqué, patchwork and quilting in a variety of cotton fabrics, inspired by a mosaic floor in Flagler College, St. Augustine, Florida

Below:
Detail from
Alchemist's Book,
by Penny Burnfield
Goldwork

Homage to British Rail
by Angela Haigh

This quilted wall-hanging (opposite) was made for Part I City and Guilds Patchwork and Quilting in 1993. Angela accompanies her husband on his railway photography trips and takes time to observe details and soak up the atmosphere. She makes sketches of railway furniture, wagons and brick walls, and records the rich feast of patterns and colours in the paintwork of old stations and their windows, roofs and arches.

She explains: 'Beneath this soaring architecture, arrows point us in all directions. We are hurried about from place to place, dominated by the clock. Few passengers have either the time or inclination to enjoy or appreciate the Victorian buildings, the tiled floors, the carved wooden barge-boards, the decorative wrought iron-work and columns, all part of our railway heritage. The quilt is a small appreciation of so much that we enjoy about railways in this country.'

Patterns on the quilted hanging include those derived from tiled floors, wooden barge-boards, the British Rail symbol, arrows, signs, brickwork, wrought iron-work, windows, the clock and the profile of the *Intercity* trains.

The reverse side (right) shows the British Rail symbol going in all directions.

Above:
Homage to British Rail,
by Angela Haigh
Reverse side

Right:
Homage to British Rail,
by Angela Haigh
127 x 102 cm
(50 x 40 in)
Patchwork, appliqué
and quilting

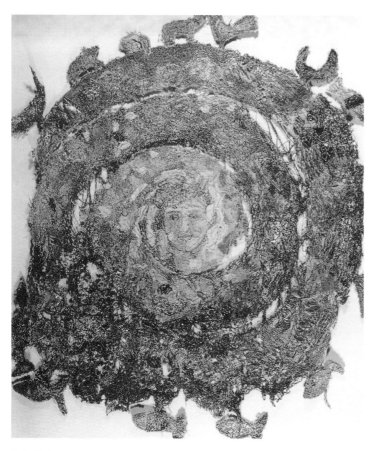

Earth Mother,
by Molly Verity
31cm (12 in) diameter
Machine embroidery on
transparent, lurex and
soluble fabrics and nets,
using metal threads

Earth Mother
by Molly Verity

The circle and the spiral are among the earliest symbols known to man, representing the sun, the moon, the movement of the stars and planets, the cycle of the seasons, the self, and eternity. 'To come full circle' was probably as meaningful in ancient times as it is now, even though the shape of the earth was not then understood. Examples of the circle and the spiral have been carved on rocks by ancient Celts all over Europe; it also appears in other forms worldwide, for example as running borders of squared spirals, in nature, Chemistry and Engineering. Women feel a real affinity to the circle, partly because of its similarity to bodily parts and partly because of their role as perpetuators of life, responsible for the daily round of family comforts and sustenance.

Molly's *Earth Mother* is the goddess in the centre of her world, benign, beautiful and all-powerful. The beasts of the field and birds of the air decorate the edges of her world, and the moon occupies the centre of it, as the female principle.

More meaningful circular shapes for your designs could come from ripples on water, planets, fruit and flowers, clock-faces, sundials, the compass, wheels and engine-parts, baskets, hats, crochet mats, tile (floor) patterns, food and ball-games.

Ring o' Roses Purse
by Jo Crouch

Ring a ring o' roses, A pocketful of posies, Atchoo! Atchoo! We all fall down.

This traditional English verse is thought to date from the time of the terrible plague of 1348, known as the Black Death, of which the first signs were carbuncles and glandular swellings, the 'ring o' roses' of the rhyme. The 'pocketful of posies' refers to the pomanders and nosegays which were used to ward off the foul smell which accompanied the disease, and the 'atchoo! atchoo!' is the sneeze which heralded the inflammation of the throat and lungs. 'We all fall down' was, of course, the usual consequence.

In Jo Crouch's pocket, long tears of grief fall off the lower edge, while rings of chain stitch and posies of flowers interpret the words.

Ring o' Roses Purse,
by Jo Crouch
20 x 18 cm (8 x 7 in) –
without fringe.
Hand-woven in slub cotton,
silk and metallic threads.
Embroidered with button-
hole-wheel flowers and
chain stitch in coloured
metal threads

Nocturne
by Jan Messent

The magical lunar hare, symbol of the
night and messenger of all nocturnal
animals, chases across the moonlit sky.
Both the moon and the hare are female
principles. Twenty-eight stars (symbolizing
woman's menstrual cycle) and four moons
(the four phases did not balance) decorate
the border. Inside, there are sixteen
nocturnal creatures (of European variety);
from top left, the owl, slow-worm, mole,
rabbit, night-jar, snail, fox, badger, toad,
bat, cat, Emperor moth, house-mouse,
hedgehog and polecat.

This piece symbolizes my love of the
country and magical things including the
moon and the hare, and the idea of social
intercourse or even conspiracy between
the creatures of the night. We humans set
so much store by what we can see, and
yet the nocturnal world is every bit as rich
to those who inhabit it; animals' senses of
smell, sound, taste and touch are finely
tuned and marvellously sensitive. Their
awareness to vibrations in the air, on the
ground and even under it make our per-
ceptions appear primitive by comparison.

Nocturne,
by Jan Messent
36 x 36 cm (14 x 14 in)
Canvaswork and surface
stitchery in wools,
silks and cottons

Gestures and Signs

Many symbolic gestures can be recognized in tapestries both ancient and modern. Some examples are given below:

Blessing: Greek, thumb and finger together. Later, third and fourth fingers folded in: thumb, first and second fingers extended to symbolize three persons of the Trinity.

Judgement: open palm.

Condemnation: single finger, pointing.

Power: Two fingers, often seen as the Hand of God emerging from the clouds.

Curved finger: speech.

Hands upraised: argument or expostulation.

Hands and arms outspread lower down: wonder, adoration, polite listening.

Legs crossed: seen as an interruption of the normal flow of life. Seen on early tomb effigies, this became an attribute of wicked emperors.

Hands clasped (variety of ways) : prayer or supplication.

The soul is always represented by a small naked figure (plus crowns, mitres, etc., to denote rank), sometimes held in a sling of fabric by a mortal or angel.

Ancient Symbols

In this miniature (right) from Gratian's *Decretum* (worked in the late Twelfth Century), the situation we see is quite serious. The lady, holding a flower as a symbol of purity, has mistakenly married the unfree serf on the left (identified by his plain garb with knotted belt, axe, unruly hair and coarse features). She should, however, have married the nobleman (tidy hair, regular features, sword and divided skirt-breeches). Quite how this came about is difficult to imagine, but she has now been released from this marriage and is taking an oath (symbolized by her left hand) on the hand of her new husband. The latter

holds his sword erect as a token of his honourable intentions. The serf looks decidedly unhappy and holds on to her sleeve in a detaining gesture while looking up at her from a bent-knee position. In view of the accurate drawing of the hands, it is difficult to believe that he is standing on the hem of her skirt by accident!

The illustration on page 124 shows a detail from the *Marian Panel*, part of the *Oxburgh Hangings*. Attributed partly to Mary, Queen of Scots, and made in around 1570, the allegorical panel was embroidered and sent to the Duke of Norfolk, whom Mary hoped to marry. The motto reads, *virescit vulnere virtus —*

'virtue flourishes by wounding' – which, on the surface, appears to imply that Mary was resigned to her imprisonment by Elizabeth. Its implicit message, however, was more likely to be that the unfruitful branch on the left (meaning Elizabeth) was to be cut down, and that Mary as the fruitful branch on the right would flourish and bear more fruit.

Could the stag (left of centre) refer to Elizabeth's love of hunting, or to herself as the hunted one? And could the windmill be a reference to the air or to the empty words of friendship, offered at a price?

Miniature from
Gratian's Decretum,
late 12th Century

Detail from the Marian
panel,
Oxburgh Hangings,
c. 1570

Four Stages in Life
by Kathleen Maclaurin

Kathleen Maclaurin lives in South Africa, though her home was once a sixteenth-century house in Kent, England. Many of the symbols used on her 'life screen' stem from her memories of England, though some of them have to do with her new family, too. Since seeing an embroidered screen at her City and Guilds class in Kent, Kathleen hankered after one of her own, seeing in the four sections a perfect vehicle for her ideas.

The first section is named *Origins* and shows a pattern of foetuses, inspired by seeing her daughter-in-law's ultra-sound scans. The second panel, named *Transient Youth*, shows swifts representing freedom, ethereal snowflakes, ephemeral butterflies, flowers and teenage pony-tails, a detail which delighted Kathleen's eldest granddaughter. The swifts overflow on to the third panel, entitled *Middle-Aged Materialism*. This shows faceless executives travelling on the freeway to the city through the empty spaces of District Six in Cape Town, where only mosques and churches remain amongst the rubble of still consecrated ground. Ghosts of the people who lived there and worked in the docks or the city are outlined in tones of grey on net which matches the background, a warm pinky-fawn Scots Craig linen.

Panel four – *Old Age: Meditation, Contemplation and Death* – shows pilgrim steps winding up through sacred symbols which represent both Christianity and Judaism. Curving from the bottom to the top, the steps worn by the countless feet of pilgrims over the centuries lead to the entrance of the Chapter House in Wells Cathedral. Kathleen remembers how she trod those same steps when serving as an unhappy W.R.N.S. driver in Bath in 1945 after having been drafted there from the beautiful Shetland Isles. The Celtic cross is from Tipperary, Ireland, her father's home, and other symbols include the Canterbury Cross and the Star of David.

Even the swifts are of personal significance; they nested in the roof of Kathleen's home in Kent each Spring. She and her husband clocked them in over a period of two days every May, and the date did not vary over twelve years. Memories indeed!

Below and overleaf:
Four Stages in Life,
by Kathleen Maclaurin
Each panel 1.65 m x 45 cm
(66 x 17 ¹/₂ in)
Appliqué and surface
stitchery

Elizabethan Symbols

The symbolism of flowers and plants was well-known to Elizabethans, hence their widespread use on embroidered articles for both personal and household use. This design is taken from a cushion of the period, the same one which Marjorie Halford used for her pale blue silk version (see page 132). Most of the plants can be identified: vetch, buttercup, hawthorn, heartsease, daffodil, bluebell, lily, gillyflower (carnation), daisy, pea, honeysuckle, strawberry, harebell and rose.

The detail from a miniature portrait of Queen Elizabeth I was made by Nicholas Hilliard, around 1595–1600. It shows arrow-heads on the ruff of lace around her neck and the symbolic crescent moon in her hair. These are symbols attributed to Diana, the chaste huntress and Moon Goddess, images of which Elizabeth was particularly fond.

Right:
Elizabethan designs

Left:
Portrait of Queen Elizabeth

The symbols to be seen on Elizabeth's clothes and in her portraits were many and various. Other favourite symbols included:

Sieve: another symbol of chastity. Tuccia, a vestal virgin, was required to prove her chastity by carrying water in a sieve, from the Tiber to the temple of the vestal virgins, without spilling a drop. Needless to say, she did.

Celestial globe: symbol of Elizabeth's expanding empire.

Pillar, spire or pyramid: symbol of constancy, support and fortitude, meaning herself.

Sword: the ancient symbol of justice.

Arrows and darts: to pierce the heart of the chaste virgin, cupid's arrows, love's darts. Also associated with Diana.

Sun-in-splendour: symbol of sovereignty.

Rainbow: promise of peace after a storm.

Non sine sol iris: 'No rainbow without a sun'.

Ears and eyes: private messages implying words of wisdom and the all-seeing eye. Sometimes sadness, especially when seen with tears.

Animals and birds were also favourite symbols, and many embroideries of the period swarmed with tiny beasts from the lowest to the most fantastic:

Ermine: another symbol of virginity. Apparently, it would rather die than soil its white fur.

Serpent: symbol of wisdom and prudence.

Pelican in Piety: legendary sources claim that it would feed its young by tearing pieces from its own breast rather than allow them to starve.

Phoenix: a huge favourite of Elizabeth, this legendary creature appealed to her particularly for its blend of uniqueness and chastity. Elizabeth was the one and only Imperial Virgin.

Of the flowers, by far Elizabeth's favourite was the eglantine, which appears on so many of her portraits. As a single white rose, it epitomized her chaste state. Other favourite flower emblems included:

Olive: this is an attribute of peace.

Spring flowers: signified that, during her reign, spring reigned eternal.

Pansy: known as heartsease, it symbolized sadness. Its name derives from the French word for thought, pensées.

One of the most fascinating pieces of embroidery belonging to the Tudor period is the *Shepherd Buss*. This is a piece of linen measuring 117 x 102 cm (46 x 41 in), embroidered in black silk. The central oval panel, showing an unhappy shepherd, is surrounded by emblems, but the great attraction of the piece is its border. This contains actual words but an emblem has been substituted for every noun, thus making the viewer work out for herself what the complete message says. It is in the Victoria and Albert Museum, London. It is well worth visiting art galleries and historic houses to see some of these wonderful embroideries for yourself.

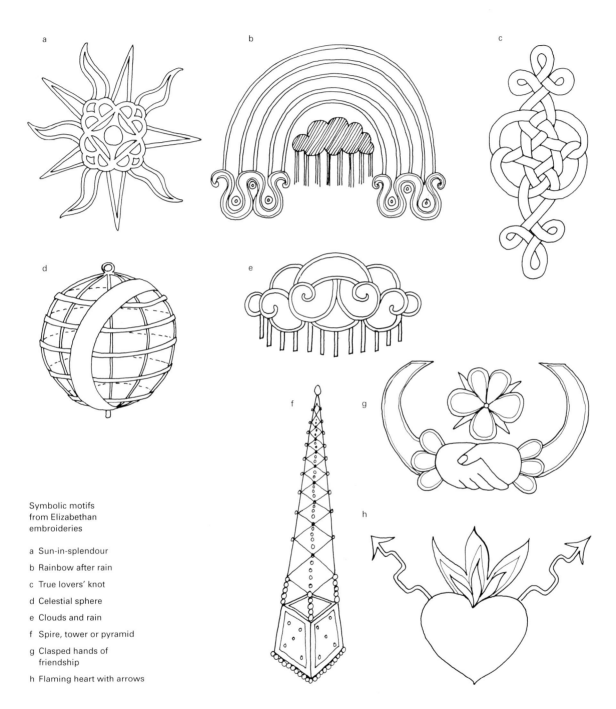

Symbolic motifs
from Elizabethan
embroideries

a Sun-in-splendour

b Rainbow after rain

c True lovers' knot

d Celestial sphere

e Clouds and rain

f Spire, tower or pyramid

g Clasped hands of
   friendship

h Flaming heart with arrows

Elizabethan Cushion,
by Marjorie Halford
46 x 46 cm (18 x 18 in)

Elizabethan Cushion
by Marjorie Halford

The design for this piece was taken from a cushion of the period, originally worked on a red satin background in silver and gilt threads. This version is delicately worked in colourful stranded silks on a pale blue silk background in padded satin stitch, French knots, stem stitch, long and short, and split stitch. The design was then quilted using reverse chain stitch.

The Quest II
by Wilcke Smith

The background for this piece is Japanese Ogura paper; tones are laid with Aquarelle crayons and overlaid with machine embroidery lace worked on dissolving fabric (U.S. Aquasolv). The figures are polymer clay, bronzed and wrapped with fibre. This is what Wilcke herself says about the piece: 'These spirits may be a metaphor for the human race adrift in eternity, seeking truths, reasons and enlightenment. I wanted a nebulous, turbulent environment filled with danger, hence the hot colours. Birds, to me, seem mystical, enigmatic messengers between the known and the unknown, so one is carried as a protector. The copper nugget symbolizes the artefacts scattered by man as he makes progress through time, and the mica disc reflects the circle of eternity.'

Eternal Guardians
by Wilcke Smith

This piece is made from hand-made paper rectangles interspersed with matching panels of padded machine whipstitch, with one recessed block almost concealing a photograph of a man who is behind a veil of silk waste. The polymer clay figures are bronzed and wrapped, and carry ritual objects: a serpent, a wand, a god's eye cruciform, a messenger bird, and an oxidized button torn loose on a battlefield in 1865. Wilcke explains: 'A guardian's work is never done, but these are not concerned with the living. They serve an intangible higher force through eternity'.

Page 134:
The Quest II,
by Wilcke Smith
31 x 23 cm (12 x 9 in)
Aquarelle crayons and
machine embroidery on
Japanese Ogura paper

Page 135:
Eternal Guardians,
by Wilcke Smith
61 x 31 cm (24 x 12 in)
Padded machine whipstich
and paper

Sun and Moon II,
by Yvonne Morton
23 x 19 cm (9 x 7 ¹/₂ in)
Machine embroidery on
hand-dyed fabrics,
mostly silk

Icons, Angels and Fools
by Yvonne Morton

The two pieces illustrated are from the series, *Icons, Angels and Fools*. They are rich in symbolism alluding to the nine orders of angels, the four elements (earth, air, fire and water), the sun and moon, the connections between heaven and earth, stars, clouds, thunder and lightning. They also contain numerical symbolism.

Flat patterns of costume have long been one of Yvonne's favourite sources of interest. Her many pieces based on kimono shapes are now superseded by those based on Eastern dress, the decoration now being concentrated on the squared inset at the neck. Traditionally a place of symbolic interest, the neckline and breast area are imbued with motifs which imply both wisdom and simple earthly things. These things relate to angels as well as fools, for fools were obliged to be astute in order to keep out of danger when their babblings were regarded as too close to the truth for comfort.

Yvonne uses machine embroidery initially, then hand-stitchery to enhance and support selected areas.

Angel's Robe
Fragment I,
by Yvonne Morton
41 x 31 cm (16 x 12 in)
Machine embroidery
on silk, some pieces
hand-dyed

Land Patterns,
by Hilary Bower
30 x 30 cm (12 x 12 in)
Machine embroidery and
hand stitchery on fabric,
paper and leather, with gold
threads and wires

**One Fish,
by Hilary Bower**
Hand-painted fabrics and
metallic braids, machine
and hand embroidery

139

Bibliography

**An Illustrated Encyclopaedia
of Traditional Symbols**
J.C. Cooper
Thames and Hudson Ltd

**Hall's Dictionary
of Subjects and Symbols in Art**
John Murray

**Embroidered Textiles – Traditional
Patterns from Five Continents**
Sheila Paine
Thames and Hudson Ltd

Drawing on the Artist Within
Betty Edwards
Fontana Collins

Blue and Yellow Don't Make Green
Michael Wilcox
Collins

Design Sources for Symbolism
Jan Messent
Crochet Design

Embroidery: A History
Pamela Warner
B.T. Batsford Ltd

Fairytale Quilts and Embroidery
Gail Harker
Merehurst Fairfax

Faces and Figures in Embroidery*
Valerie Campbell-Harding
B.T. Batsford Ltd

**Brewer's Dictionary
of Phrase and Fable**
Cassell

Roget's Thesaurus
Penguin
(or any other Thesaurus)

* This book is out of print, but you should
be able to obtain a copy from your local
library or second-hand book dealer.

Index

Illustrations are italicized.